Dream Interpretation
From
Classical Jewish Sources

Dream Interpretation
From
Classical Jewish Sources

by
Rabbi Shelomo Almoli

Translated and Annotated by
Yaakov Elman

KTAV PUBLISHING HOUSE, INC.

Library of Congress Cataloging-in-Publication Data

Almoli, Solomon ben Jacob. 15th/16th cent.
    [Pitron ḥalomot. English]
    Dream interpretation from classical Jewish sources / by Shelomo Almoli ;
translated and annotated by Yaakov Elman.
    p. cm.
    Includes bibliographical references.
    ISBN 0-88125-533-5
    1. Dream interpretation in rabbinical literature—Early works to 1800.
2. Dreams—Religious aspects—Judaism—Early works to 1800. I. Elman,
Yaakov. II. Title.
BF1075.A413   1998
154.6'34'089924—dc21   98-12315
                                                                    CIP

Manufactured in the United States of America
KTAV Publishing House, 900 Jefferson Street, Hoboken NJ, 07030

Contents

Translator's Introduction

Dreams were a recognized medium of prophecy throughout the Biblical era, and are well known in the Bible. Their importance was recognized not only by the Israelites but in the cultures around them; indeed, one of the earliest works of dream interpretation is the so-called *Assyrian Dream Book,* dating from at least the ninth century B.C.E.[1] While the precursors of this work date back perhaps another thousand years, dreams and their interpretations are mentioned in Sumerian and Akkadian texts from long before that. Later, during Hellenistic and Roman times, dream interpretation continued to play an important role, with several systematic works on dreams and their interpretations by classical authors such as Macrobius and Artemidorus, the largest and most complete. Artemidorus lists some 3,000 dreams![2]

Among the Jews, the end of the prophetic era did not mark the end of prophecy, or of prophetic dreams.

> Said R. Avdimi of Haifa: Since the day the Temple was destroyed, prophecy was taken from the prophets and given to the Sages.[3]

While prophecy here is not specifically limited to dreams, the Talmud reports on many prophetic dreams dreamed by various sages, most of which were examined and discussed by R. Solomon Almoli in his book, a translation of which appears below. Such concerns did not cease in the sixteenth century, however, and with the rise of Hasidism in the eighteenth and nineteenth centuries more and more notice was taken of dreams and their interpretation. A number of hasidic teachers are known to have kept track of their dreams, and these constitute a remarkable and valuable spiritual record. Among them are R. Yitzhak Yehudah Yehiel of Komarno (1806–1874) and R. Zadok ha-Kohen of Lublin (1823–1900). Dream interpretation has continued into the twentieth century as well, as the works of R. Judah Moses Ftayya of Baghdad (1859–1943) attest.[4]

Despite all the concern with dreams and their interpretation over thousands of years, one work stands out for its completeness and thorough analysis, the *Pitron Halomot* of R. Solomon Almoli. It has been reprinted many times since its initial publication in 1515, and various adaptations have appeared in the twentieth century, one as recently as 1965. It is R. Almoli's work which appears below in translation.

R. Isaac de Leon, author of the classic commentary *Megillat Esther* on Maimonides' *Sefer ha-Mitzvot,* thought sufficiently highly of R. Solomon Almoli to quote him in the introduction to his own work. While it was R. Almoli's fate not to have completed the works he had begun, and to be forgotten after his death, it was also his good fortune to produce one book that became an "underground" classic, a work that was reprinted many times, both in the form in which he issued it and in modified form or translation, sometimes attributed to him and sometimes not.

Born in the 1480s in Spain and orphaned at a young age, R. Almoli reached Constantinople by 1516, where he served as a judge of one of the rabbinic courts, and possibly as a rabbi as well, but apparently made his living as a physician. He planned to write an encyclopedic work which would present the reader with a compendium of all that was new and noteworthy in human knowledge, *Me'assef le-Khol ha-Mahanot,* but little of it was ever published. Aside from his well-known treatise on dream interpretation, he also wrote a book on Hebrew grammar, *Halikhot Sheva.* He also was instrumental in having a number of other grammatical works published, among them Ibn Ezra's *Safah Berurah* and Ibn Yahya's *Leshon Limmudim.*[5]

In his work on dream interpretation, originally titled *Mefashhar Helmin,* and published in Salonika in 1515, R. Almoli follows the same plan that governed his approach to his other work, collecting all the reliable sources he could find on the subject, carefully analyzing them, and arranging them according to topic. As he states in his preface,

> In the poverty of my knowledge, I had not studied this wisdom, and was unacquainted with it. Seeing my incapacity, I decided to collect a number of treatises on the subject, in particular those incorporated into our holy volumes of Talmud, the holy Zohar, the dream interpretations of R. Saadiah Gaon, R. Hai Gaon, and others.
>
> Thus, even though the treatises included here were each composed by a different author, they are arranged as though by one writer. This is because each selection deals with a particular topic, and the one following supplements and explains the preceding one. I, for my part, have not added anything of my own, but merely quote what has already been written, with full credit given to the author. I take no credit for myself, since, as it has been said, anthologizing is merely the expenditure of labor, but not wisdom itself.[6]

R. Almoli is too modest in not claiming credit for himself, for his account of dreams contains a large amount of analysis of conflicting sources and evaluation of various theories. Among the authorities he quotes are the Bible, the Talmud and Zohar, the Rambam and Ramban, both Avraham Ibn Ezra and Moshe Ibn Ezra, R. Isaac Arama (author of *Akedat Yitzhak*), R. Eleazar of Worms (known as the Rokeah), and philosophical works like the Ralbag's *Milhamot Hashem,* Aristotle's *On Sense and Sensible Objects* and *On the Soul,* as well as Averroes, the Muslim commentator on Aristotle, Avicenna, the Muslim philosopher, and Al-Ghazzali, the Persian one.[7] Clearly, R. Almoli must have gone to great lengths to obtain whatever had ever been written on dream interpretation.

The book does not read like a patchwork, however, because R. Almoli's analytic and organizational abilities combined all these sources into a workable, if not harmonious, whole. Unfortunately, however, his style and descriptive abilities were not equal to his organizational ones; aside from occasional awkward sentences whose meaning is difficult to extract, he tends to repeat himself. Also, because of his desire to include nearly everything pertinent to his subject, he often piles on proof after proof, when one or two would be enough. As a consequence, the following translation occasionally omits these repetitive proofs, though nothing of the essential arguments he makes has been left out. Furthermore, though the translation is generally literal, R. Almoli's syntax has often been simplified.

NOTES

[1] See A. L. Oppenheim, *The Interpretation of Dreams in the Ancient Near East,* Transactions of the American Philosophical Society, New Series, 46/3 (Philadelphia: American Philosophical Society, 1956). Among its other merits, it contains an exhaustive discussion of ancient dream interpretation.

[2] See E. R. Dodds, *The Greeks and the Irrational* (Berkeley and Los Angeles: University of California Press, 1951), esp. chap. IV, "Dream-Pattern and Culture-Pattern," pp. 102–134. See also his *Pagan and Christian in an Age of Anxiety: Some Aspects of Religious Experience from Marcus Aurelius to Constantine* (Cambridge: Cambridge University Press, 1965).

[3] Bava Batra 12a.

[4] An excerpt will be found in the appendices.

[5] See H. Alon's edition of *Halikhot Sheva* (Jerusalem: Mosad Harav Kook, 1944), p. 81.

[6] See p. XX below.

[7] For a study of his sources, see A. Gruenbaum, *Pitron Halomot: Korot u-Mekorot, Areshet* 4 (5726), pp. 180–201.

First Treatise

On the Science of Dream Interpretation

Says the author: When I beheld the precious dignity of this work, its priceless research, dearer than gold, its great usefulness for all, whether young or old, and its clarity, for with it everyone will understand how to interpret dreams, I said to myself that the time had come to publish it and send it out to all the boundaries of Israel, in order that those who read it and meditate on it may increase.[1]

We human beings always wish to know the truth about everything, especially regarding propitious and unpropitious events which are destined to occur. Since we do not have sufficient understanding to apprehend it all in a perfect manner, God has provided ways to inform us of these matters, either by means of a prophetic vision or by means of a dream. Indeed, little occurs in the world which is not announced from Above in some manner.

This point is stated in the Zohar:

> Come and see: there is nothing which comes to the world without having been announced in a dream or by means of a messenger, as it was taught: Everything is announced in Heaven before it comes to the world; from there it spreads throughout the world and is given over by a messenger, as is written: "The Lord God does nothing without revealing His secret to His servants, the prophets"[2]—at the time when there were prophets. And even when prophetic inspiration is lacking, there are "Sages who are superior to prophets,"[3] and even when no dream is granted, matters are revealed and ordained through the birds of heaven.[4]

Although we have been exiled from our land, and both prophecy and the Urim and Tumim [in the high priest's breastplate, with which the future success

5

or failure of public decisions was forecast,] have been hidden away, nevertheless there remains the Divine grace[5] of simple dreams, by which we are informed of all such matters. This was stated by our Sages: Said Rava: Even though "I will surely hide My Face from them on that day,"[6] says the Holy One, blessed be He, "I will speak to him by means of a dream,"[7] as has been explained.[8] In spite of this, dreams are useless, since they are beyond our understanding and none of us knows how to interpret them. This lack of understanding proceeds from several causes. These include our inability to understand the strange metaphors in which dreams are clothed and the great number of different forms that these parables take. In addition, few people are both imaginative enough and sufficiently aware of the dreamer's affairs to be able to properly interpret these images. Moreover, there is an admixture of nonsense in dreams, and finally, some dreams really are of no consequence. For all these reasons it is impossible to put these matters down in writing except in the most general terms; the details are forever hidden from the interpreter, and there is no way to know them but by conjecture. Thus in most cases it is impossible to engage in dream interpretation without error.

In this regard Abuhamad[9] is correct when he writes that in the nature of the matter, dream interpretation is impossible except by means of conjecture, and as a result error is predominant in such activities. And even though there is no niggardliness Above to limit or deprive us of this grace, we lack [knowledge of how to interpret dreams] due to our deficiencies and negligence in acquiring an understanding of these matters.

It is as Elihu said in the Book of Job, "For God speaks once, twice—though man does not perceive it—in a dream, in a night vision, when deep sleep falls on men, when they slumber in their beds; then He opens men's understanding, and by disciplining them, leaves His signet."[10] From God's point of view, He has opened men's understanding, but from our point of view the manner of "opening" is sealed and closed, with no one to understand. That is the meaning of "and by disciplining them, He leaves his signet"—since they refuse discipline and do not wish to understand the dreams, He seals their future affairs. This is done to such an extent that it is a reason "to turn man away from an action, to suppress the essence[11] in a man."[12] This is to be interpreted in reverse, as though the verse stated: "to remove the action of a man," that is to say, "that the action which is hinted in it [i.e., the dream] will be removed from the man's understanding."

As a result, it was customary in ancient times for people to pursue knowledge of this and ancillary sciences on their own; a person with a dream would consult such an expert, and would be informed of the import of his dream. Doing this was not considered a vain activity, since it is impossible for everyone to be expert in these matters, but only "one in a city, two in a clan"[13]—and even so, the matter remained doubtful.

That is how things stood [in ancient times], with men like Joseph, Daniel, R. Ishmael, Bar Hadaya, and the twenty-four dream interpreters of Jerusalem mentioned in the Talmud.[14] As to the latter, the plenitude of Divine inspiration there was the reason so many dream interpreters were found in one place,[15] since the Divine Presence and the ark of the covenant were located in Jerusalem. That is why so many highly accomplished dream interpreters were to be found in Jerusalem, as R. Nehorai noted.[16]

And so too there were experts in every generation who would study this science and know its methods, so as to inform people of the interpretations of their dreams, though not all of them were worthy. This may have been what Joseph meant when he told Pharaoh that "the interpretations are a Sage's,"[17] as the word *elohim* may be so understood, and so too "I say that you are Sages."[18] The verse in Genesis being understood as stating that such interpretations are the province of Sages.

However, the difficulty of mastering this science is the reason for its removal from humankind, until, due to our many sins, we have reached a time when the word of God is rare and visions are not interpreted.[19]

It seems to me that this is what the prophet Isaiah hinted at when he said, "Act stupid, and be stupefied!"[20] He was warning us of what will result from an utter lack of knowledge of this science: knowledge of dream interpretation will be totally lost, even when books setting forth the methods of interpretation are available. That this verse speaks of interpreting dreams may be proven from the adjacent verses, which begin "Then, like a dream, a vision of the night . . . like one who dreams . . ."[21]

While these verses may be explicated as the classical commentators understood them, they may also be explained as relating to the knowledge of dream interpretation, as I will explain, and even more so than the standard interpretation.

This then is the proper understanding. In the past [before Isaiah's time] the science of dream interpretation had been perfected and all were expert in it, as we have stated; it was a matter of great wonderment to the prophet that in his time no one knew anything of this wisdom, and so he began his prophecy by saying, "Act stupid, and be stupefied!"[22] In other words, think long and hard about this, in order to grasp it thoroughly, and once you do, you too will wonder how such a thing can be—how it is possible for future occurrences to come to pass as I have predicted.

And he also says "Speak among yourselves and speak!"[23] from the Rabbinic Aramaic word *mishta'ei*. What he means is: Consider the subject yourself and speak to others about it—about how I am able to speak of future events. Or perhaps he means: "Refrain from speech" in order to consider the matter, and only afterwards discuss the question of the prophesying of future events. That is, he was so convinced of the truth of what he foretold that it was as if it had already come to pass, and therefore his prophecies are all related in the past tense even though they were meant for the future.[24] This is what is written further on: "They are drunk, but not from wine; they stagger, but not from liquor."[25] In other words, they are so far from knowledge that even when they are sober they are like drunkards who do not know right from left. Isaiah explains their ignorance as follows: "For God has spread over you a spirit of deep sleep";[26] this means that they are devoid of Divine or prophetic inspiration, which comes to a man during a time of deep sleep, in a dream or a vision of the night. God will hide it from you so that you do not understand it, close your eyes so that you do not perceive it. How so? He hides these matters by means of symbol and metaphor, visions and riddles that are not understood. And so too your leaders, the seers[27] and those who delve into books of dream interpretation and interpret them to others according to what they see in them—they too will not understand; from all these the Holy One, blessed be He, has hidden this knowledge so that it should not be understood.

"So that all prophecy shall be to you as the words of a sealed book."[28] That is, there are people whose dreams are understandable to others, in keeping with their degree of insight, and the prophet states about this that "all prophecy shall be to you as the words of a sealed book."

In other words, there are two types of interpreters: those who study books of dream interpretation and are familiar with their details, and those who have not studied such books, but interpret dreams by the power of insight and imagination. Now, members of these two categories mentioned by the prophet will admit their ignorance. Those who have book knowledge will say that the book is sealed, and those who do not will admit that they have no access to such books.

The prophet also explains why the Holy One, blessed be He, has hidden these matters from Israel: they are akin to prophecy, and thus come only to those who fear God and esteem His Name.[29] As the Sages have said, Anyone who goes seven days without a dream is called evil, etc.[30] This is because he is like one who "honors Me with his mouth and lips"[31]—which is the essence, since God desires the heart—but "his heart he has distanced from Me,"[32] and "thus I will further confuse that people with confusion upon confusion."....[33]

And this, then, is why he concludes his prophecy with "and the wisdom of its wise shall fail, and the discernment of its discerning ones will be hidden."[34] The latter refers to one like Joseph, who is called "discerning" by Pharaoh.[35] The two categories, wise and discerning, advert to what we discussed above: those who study books of dream interpretation, and those who understand dreams on their own. The first are called "wise," the second, "discerning."

Clearly, all this refers to those previous generations, for "now the people of the land are many, who do not know or understand, who go in darkness"[36] regarding dream interpretation—so much so that knowledge of this subject is nearly completely lacking among us, and the little that remains is of so little use that it is as though it did not exist. I wonder at the early Sages,[37] who composed volumes on each and every rabbinic comment, and yet not one of them wrote a single book on this topic.

From the Talmud it seems that Bar Hadaya[38] did possess a special work on this, as we read that "a book fell from him and Rava found it. He saw written within that 'All dreams follow their interpretation.'"[39] Thus, I find it quite strange that people disparage dreams as nonsense—so much so that they refer to any nonsense as "dreams."

And so when I, Solomon Almoli, the most insignificant of my generation, saw all this, I became zealous for the God of Hosts and for His people Israel, in order that this knowledge not be completely lost from us. Therefore I decided to delve into all the ways of this science, as described by scholars and written in books; and to compose a work containing their words, whether many or few, in accordance with my meager understanding, with "one small spoon"[40] which shall flower like a rose and will in the end become a portion unto the whole people, for it is time to be gracious unto her.[41]

I have called this book "Dream Interpreter," because its essential purpose is to provide true methods and principles by which everyone can know how to interpret dreams and understand their intent. The reader will understand the details of every dream anyone may have, that is, what each dream signifies. [A secondary purpose of the book is] to provide means by which evil dreams may be rectified or annulled, mitigating their evil. In addition, [I have provided] the laws pertaining to dreams, since their purpose is to rectify and annul evil dreams and dilute their evil.[42] Therefore, we have divided the first part of the book into three parts: the first is intended to guide prospective interpreters to an understanding of the purpose of dreams; the second deals with the actual interpretations—what each element symbolizes; the third part presents the [religious] laws governing them, so that every evil dream may be rectified and annulled after it is dreamed.

[The first part of the book] is divided into eight gates. The first gate is devoted to defining what a dream is and to classifying various types of dreams and the differences between them. The second investigates whether or not dreams are reliable; the third explains the signs by which true prophetic dreams may be recognized; the fourth tells about those things that usually appear in dreams and those that do not; the fifth discusses the three basic principles an interpreter must know in order to interpret dreams properly; the sixth explains that every dream must be interpreted in the context of the dreamer's work and lifestyle. The seventh gate explains whether dreams follow the interpretation or not—included therein is a long analysis that will clarify this matter. The eighth gate explains how to determine the time when a dream will be fulfilled, whether sooner or later.

Gate One

Defining the dream and its distinctive categories.

Chapter One explains the definition and types, Chapter Two the differences between them.

Chapter One

There are three types of dreams, one of higher rank than the other. The highest are the dreams of prophets, such as the dreams of Jacob,[43] Daniel,[44] and Solomon[45]—all these were certainly prophetic dreams [because they came to individuals who were prophets], as the Biblical narrative clearly demonstrates. And even though Maimonides maintains in his *Guide of the Perplexed* II:45 that Daniel and Solomon are not considered to have been prophets, he admits that they achieved at least the minimum level of prophecy, which is known as Divine inspiration (*ruah ha-kodesh*). Thus, their dreams are regarded as having been on a higher level than ordinary dreams, which are themselves considered a sixtieth part of prophecy.[46]

The second category is that of ordinary dreams,[47] such as those of Joseph,[48] Pharaoh,[49] the Chief Cupbearer[50] and Chief Baker,[51] as well as those of Avimelekh[52] and Laban the Aramean.[53] All of these were ordinary dreams, for as Maimonides points out, it is impossible that Laban the Aramean, who was a completely wicked idol-worshiper, and Avimelekh, of whose land and kingdom Abraham commented that "there is no fear of the Lord in this place,"[54] could have attained the level of prophecy.[55] . . . [56]

The third category is that of the sorcerous dreams of false prophets, regarding which the Torah says, "or one who dreams a dream,"[57] or, as Jeremiah says, "I have heard what the false prophets prophesy in My Name, falsely saying, 'I have dreamed, I have dreamed,' who try to cause My people to forget My Name by their dreams which they tell one another."[58] The category is represented by Shemaiah the Nechelmite, who, in my view, was called "Nechalmi" because he would induce these dreams by his own efforts. In all of these instances, the words and phrases describing the dreams prove without doubt that they were neither prophetic nor ordinary, but rather sorcerous.

These then are the three categories of dreams. It may be that Elihu[59] referred to all three when he said, "For God speaks in one way, and in two, though man does not perceive it; in a dream, a night vision, when deep sleep falls on men, while they slumber on their beds. Then He opens man's understanding, and by disciplining them leaves His signature—to turn man away from an action, to suppress pride in a man."[60] . . . Regarding the first category [prophetic dreams] he says, "in a dream, a night vision"; this refers to a prophetic dream like Jacob's, which is explicitly described as "visions of the night."[61] Regarding ordinary dreams he says, "when deep sleep falls on men," since it is known that ordinary dreams occur after the dreamer falls into a deep sleep of his own accord. Of the third category, he says, "when they slumber on their beds," since sorcerous dreams come by the dreamer's own choice inasmuch as he induces them by what he does as he prepares himself for sleep, and thus it might be said that the dreamer brings them on by means of conjuration.[62]

[After listing the three categories, Elihu] explains each one of them. Regarding the first, he says, "Then He opens man's understanding," that is, by means of a prophetic dream He provides morally perfect men with absolute knowledge. Regarding the second, "by disciplining them leaves His signature," that is to say, [ordinary dreams] are not like prophetic dreams, which are crystal clear, but are hidden and obscure, since men are removed[63] from understanding them. Regarding the third he says, "to turn man away from an action," that is, although sorcerous dreams are not true, God gives them a place in His scheme of things so that we may understand their essential falsity and remove ourselves from that action and that arrogance, "to suppress pride in a man." Hence, all three categories are referred to here.

Chapter Two

The distinctions between these categories have now been discussed; despite our ignorance of the prerequisite knowledge needed for a full understanding of this subject, we are obligated to investigate it as far as our limited knowledge allows. . . .

The first distinction is that a prophetic dream comes only to one who is wise, righteous, valiant, and wealthy, as our Sages noted.[64] Dreams of the other two categories come to anyone, even if he lacks these qualities, and whether or not he is [morally] prepared for the dream, as was the case with Joseph, Pharaoh's Chief Cupbearer, and Pharaoh's Chief Baker.

The second distinction: even though a prophetic dream comes by means of the influence of an angel, as Maimonides said,[65] the angel is not seen but comes with God. God speaks His words to the angel and the angel repeats them to the prophet, in the manner of every prophecy, since prophecy is impossible without the presence of God. We know this because we find this condition in all prophetic dreams. Thus, in the case of Jacob, "Behold, angels of God were ascending and descending the ladder, and God stood over him, and He said. . . ."[66] In other instances, however, even though the dreams come from God, there is no mention of God's presence, as in the cases of Avimelekh and Laban the Aramean. . . . It would seem that this distinction is referred to in the Talmud's comment on the verse "I will certainly hide My Face from them on that day" [in the first chapter of Hagigah]. "Said Rava: 'Even though I will hide My Face from them on that day,' said the Holy One, blessed be He, 'In a dream will I speak to him,'[67] and this is how the Sages interpreted the term 'Face' mentioned in the verse as referring to prophecy, as is written, 'Face to face God spoke [to you],'"[68] . . . . The reason is that [prophetic dreams] do not come to a person only through the medium of an angel, but the Holy One, blessed be He, comes Himself and in His Glory, with His angels and servitors, who perform His will, in order to inform the prophet of the prophecy which He wishes to impart, as this is described in most cases of this sort. Thus, it would seem that what God hides from them in their exile is God's Presence [i.e., His Face], by means of which prophecy comes to the prophet, [but not more ordinary clairvoyant dreams], which come only by means of an angel. . . .[69]

Furthermore, even if most of a prophet's dreams are in fact prophetic, it is not impossible that he will often have ordinary dreams. . . . Sometimes, when they are not prepared for a prophetic vision, they have ordinary dreams. . . .

The third distinction is the one noted by R. Ibn Hasdai[70] in chapter 13, 24:2 of his book:[71] a prophetic dream differs from an ordinary one in respect to the strength or weakness of the impression it makes on the prophet's imagination. Put differently, the impression on the imaginative faculty is so intense that the prophet remembers what he dreamed, never forgetting it, as if he had seen it when awake. In contrast, an ordinary dream comes when the imaginative faculty is weak, and in consequence one sometimes forgets what he dreams, as in the case of Nebuchadnezzar and Pharaoh, where some details were lost in Pharaoh's retelling of the dream to Joseph in comparison with the description given by the Torah, which is of course the accurate depiction. . . . [72]

The fourth distinction: in a prophetic dream [the essential prophecy] is presented by means of an image or a parable, and as Maimonides explains in chapter 7 of Hilkhot Yesodei ha-Torah, the prophet immediately understands the import of the image or parable. In contrast, the meaning of an ordinary dream is infinitely hidden and obscure. This is hinted in the words of Elihu cited above, "Then He opens man's understanding, and by disciplining them leaves His signet," as I have already explained. And in regard to Avimelekh's dream, where the Torah explicitly states "He [i.e., God] said to him," it appears to me that this is not to be taken literally, but instead indicates that he was shown these matters by means of images which hinted at the meaning intended; the Torah, however, did not wish to describe any of this at length.

The fifth distinction: there is nothing nonsensical in a prophetic dream; quite the contrary, every detail is significant, as in the dreams of Jacob[73] and Solomon.[74] . . .

In the Zohar it states:

R. Yose opened his discourse with the following, saying: "Just as dreams come with much concern, so does foolish utterance come with much speech."[75] Just as dreams come with much concern—it has already explained this as applying to the fact that [dreams may be categorized] in various layers (semikhin) and levels. Some dreams are entirely true, and some have an admixture of truth and falsehood. But as to those righteous ones, no false matters are revealed to them at all, but all are true. See what is written [in regard to Daniel]: "There was the secret utterly revealed to Daniel in a vision of the night."[76] If there were false matters admixed, why was it included[77] in the Holy Writings? Rather, for the righteous, when their souls ascend, only holy matters adhere to them and they are informed only of matters of truth and verity which will never be uprooted.[78]

Thus, in contrast to other categories of dreams, there is no nonsense whatsoever in any elevated dream of a high level of spirituality, a prophetic dream, etc.

Now that we have presented the five differences between prophetic and non-prophetic dreams, we proceed to the differences between [prophetic dreams] and the two remaining categories [ordinary and sorcerous dreams], in regard to which there are four distinctions.

First, ordinary dreams, which come to most people, originate through Divine influence, by the mediation of His angels, valiant of strength, who fulfill His will, and serve before Him on His right hand,[79] but sorcerous dreams come from His left hand[80] by the mediation of demons and liliths. Regarding them Scripture says: "Behold, I am against those prophets of false dreams whom I have not sent or commanded,"[81] and further, "Those who plan to cause My people to forget My Name with the dreams which they tell."[82]

In the Zohar it is stated:

R. Hiyya opened his discourse and said: "Hear these My words: When a prophet of God arises among you, I make Myself known to him in a vision, I speak with him in a dream."[83] Come and see how many degrees and subdivisions did the Holy One, blessed be He, make; each stands one above the other, degree upon degree, one above the other, and all receive their [spiritual] sustenance as you see, these from the Right and these from the Left. These are each appointed on these below them, as is proper. Come and see that all the prophets derive their [spiritual] sustenance from one side of the two known sides, and those degrees are seen through the mirror which is not clear, as is written, "I make Myself known to him in a vision."[84] What is that? As is said: they see that all aspects appear in it, and that is the mirror which is not clear. "In a dream I will speak to him"[85]—this is one-sixtieth of prophecy, as the Sages interpreted, and that is the sixth degree of that degree of prophecy, which is the degree of Gabriel, who is the one appointed over dreams.[86]

Likewise, in chapter 9 of tractate Berakhot; "Rava pointed out the following contradiction: 'In a dream I speak to him,'[87] but it is also written, 'They speak vain dreams.'[88] However, there is no difficulty; one refers to dreams which come through the mediation of an angel, and the other to those which come through a demon."[89] . . . .

Second, there is no ordinary dream which does not have some truth in it, whether great or small, in contrast to sorcerous dreams, all or most of which are false. . . . And in Genesis Rabba: "Said R. Abbahu: 'Dream messages are of no account.'[90] [However, it is told that] a certain person came to R. Yose b. Halafta and said to him: 'It was said to me in a dream: "Go fetch your father's bailment in Cappadocia.'" 'Was your father ever in Cappadocia?' the latter asked. 'No.' 'If so, count to the tenth beam of your house and there you will find it.' 'I don't have ten beams in my house.' 'In that case, count from beginning to end and back, and there you will find it.' He went, did so, and found it, and from this R. Yose b. Halafta learned that which Bar Kappara taught: 'There is no dream without its correct interpretation.'"[91] We see from this that while R. Abbahu held dreams of no account, the Midrash cites an incident which contradicts this view, cited as well in the teachings of Bar Kappara. . . .

Third, an ordinary dream is not willed by the dreamer, for it comes, not by his choice, but by the Will of God, while a sorcerous dream comes by the dreamer's own choice and volition, as determined by the spells and incubations he uses to summon the demon that shows him the answer to his request by means of imaginings, as the prophet Jeremiah said: "Do not listen to their dreams which they cause themselves to dream."[92]

For the fourth distinction, see Gate Three; however, sorcerous dreams are all equal, in accordance with the dreamer's knowledge of [demonic] names and expertise in this craft. Thus you have four distinctions in this as well, in order to distinguish between pure and impure. This being so, there are only two types of true dreams, the prophetic and the common. . . . [93]

Gate Two

Gate Two, which discusses whether or not it is proper to rely on ordinary dreams, is divided into three chapters. The first demonstrates that there are conflicting views on this question; the second, that the view that dreams are reliable and true and a minor form of prophecy is correct; and the third explains the contradictions cited in the first chapter.

Chapter One

Chapter One demonstrates that opinions differ on this question. As we have seen, Scripture says: "I will speak to him in a dream,"[94] and the whole Torah is full of dreams of this kind. This indicates that dreams may be relied upon and are true and reliable. Indeed, even though Joseph's dreams were not fully prophetic, we find that they were nevertheless fulfilled to the utmost degree. Even what he dreamed about the moon, [which was to bow to him,[95] and] which denoted his mother [Rachel, who died before the dream could be fulfilled], was fulfilled in regard to Bilhah, who [after Rachel's death] raised him as a mother. And similarly the first of these dreams[96] was not in vain, but was fulfilled on another occasion, as will be explained in the Fifth Gate, with God's help. Moreover, we find that dreams are correct, true, and reliable in regard to righteous and wicked alike. Thus, the wicked Pharaoh dreamed about seven cows and seven ears, and the interpretation regarding the seven years of plenty and the seven years of famine came to him, of which it was stated, "that which the Lord does He showed Pharaoh."[97] There is no doubt that the seven years of plenty occurred in Egypt, and so too would the seven years of famine, had it not been for the merit of Jacob, whose arrival in Egypt caused five years to be subtracted, as our Sages explain.[98] So too were the dreams of the Chief Baker and the Chief Butler fulfilled—"as he [i.e., Joseph] interpreted for them, so it was."[99] And similarly all of Nebuchadnezzar's dreams were fulfilled; hence our proofs from Scripture.

Our Sages also said in Chapter "He Who Sees"[100] that dreams are a one-sixtieth part of prophecy.[101] And in Genesis Rabba: "Dreams are a shadow of prophecy."[102] We see likewise that our Sages were careful in regard to dreams, as in the first chapter of tractate Taanit:[103] "R. Samuel[104] b. Onio[105] and R. Huna b. Manoah and R. Hiyya of Wastanya frequently attended Rava's lectures. When Rava died they went to those of R. Papa. Whenever he stated a law which did not seem logical to them they would glance[106] at one another, and this bothered him greatly. In a dream the verse 'And I cut off the three shepherds in one month'[107] was recited before him. The next day he said to them: Let the Rabbis go to peace."[108] There are so many similar stories that they said in Chapter "He Who Sees": "Anyone who has a dream that makes him sad should go and have it sweetened. . . ."[109] And in the first chapter of tractate Shabbat [11a] and also in the first chapter of tractate Taanit [12b] "we say that fasting is as effective [in combating a bad] dream as fire is [in igniting] tow," to which R. Hisda added [that the fast must be carried out] on the selfsame day, and R. Yosef added, even on the Sabbath [when fasting is ordinarily forbidden].

Moreover, the Sages of the Talmud debated the various types of dreams at great length in order to explain how they could be interpreted and what each denoted, but if dreams are not efficacious, what was the point of their doing all this?

There is no need to expatiate on the question with numerous proofs. Experience alone suffices to verify that this is true, for it is not at all uncommon for dreams to be fulfilled, so much so, in fact, that the dreamer realizes that the situation he is experiencing was foreshadowed in his dream. Obviously, then, dreams are efficacious and reliable, and one should take care regarding them.

However, other sources seem to indicate the very opposite: Scripture states that "as for dreams, they speak vanity,"[110] and furthermore, "a dream comes from much brooding,"[111] and our Sages, may their memory be blessed, state [at the end of tractate] Horiyot in tractate Sanhedrin, and in midrashim that dream matters have no effect. Furthermore, there are everyday instances of dreams not being fulfilled; even when the dream is interpreted and the interpretation is known,[112] it is still not fulfilled, neither in the way it was interpreted nor in any similar manner.

Indeed, Samuel himself seems to have been in doubt on this matter, for the Talmud reports that whenever Samuel had a bad dream he would say, "As for dreams, they speak vanity,"[113] and when he had a favorable dream he would say in a questioning tone, "they speak vanity?" But is it not written "In a dream I speak to him"?[114]

Chapter Two

Chapter Two is devoted to explaining which direction to take in this debate; and on this I will say, after careful consideration, that the absolute truth appears to inhere in the opinion that dreams are correct and true, and are close to prophecy. In order to explain fully, I have divided this chapter into two parts. The first explains and verifies, from several points of view and with several proofs, that this means of communication is Divine, issuing from the Divine grace of God in Heaven. The second explains why dreams come while the dreamer is asleep and not when he is awake. . . . [115]

Chapter Three

Chapter Three is devoted to reconciling the contradictions raised in Chapter One.

Behold, in the gate following this one [Gate Three] I will explain the four conditions necessary for a dream to be accurate, and without which it is inaccurate. This will reconcile all the contradictions in Chapter One. Sometimes a dream meets all these conditions and thus is absolutely correct, while other times only some conditions are met and the dream is of middling accuracy. For this reason every dream should be tested by means of these criteria in order to determine whether it is accurate or not.

Gate Three

Gate Three explains the differences between true and untrue dreams; it is divided into five chapters, elaborating in turn the differences resulting from the [dreamer's spiritual status], the foods he has eaten, the dreamer's thoughts, the time of the dream, and finally, the effect on the dreamer.

Chapter One

Chapter One, regarding the differences among individuals in regard to dreams, is divided into two sections, the first pertaining to astrological signs, the second, to [spiritual] degree.

Dreams differ in accordance with the dreamer's astrological sign . . . , but since I am not a master of this art, I have not treated these matters at length; besides which, as Jews we must believe that astrological factors only increase the probability of a given outcome but do not absolutely determine it.

The second section explains that we are informed of future events in accordance with our [spiritual] degree. The philosophers maintain that dream prophecies are more suited to young people and fools than to educated adults, as Gersonides[116] wrote.

This is because fools and the young do not exert their senses to achieve new insights or to amass scattered knowledge. Their imaginative faculty is quiescent when they are awake, and operates according to its wont when they are asleep, assembling disconnected facts. As a result, during the hours of sleep it imagines true and correct matters of future import.

In my opinion this view is wrong, because it issues from the fundamental, and untenable, assumption that dreams are not of Divine origin. In our view, insofar as we believe that dreams are of Divine origin, we hold that the dreams of adults and the educated are more accurate than those of fools and the young. This is because individuals who occupy themselves with metaphysical questions come closer and closer to God, may He be blessed, and in doing so become ever more fit recipients for Divine inspiration, so that they dream true prophetic

21

dreams. Note that Ibn Sinna [Avicenna][117] agrees with us on one point: that the young do not dream.

In any case, in our opinion the quality of dreams varies with the dreamer's [spiritual] level, and this is also the opinion of the Zohar:

R. Yose opened his discourse and said: "'For the dream comes from much concern.'[118] Behold, this has been interpreted to mean that dreams may be categorized in various layers and levels." Moreover, there is also written: "The Holy One, blessed be He, informs people of these matters each according to his degree and in the manner appropriate for each one [according to his degree], each matter certainly comes to the person most appropriate for that revelation. Come and see that when a person lies on his bed, his soul issues forth and roams the upper world, entering into whatever place it enters, and various bands of pure [spirits] move to and fro in these worlds and meet that [wandering] soul, which sees what it sees; however, if not, it takes hold of that side,[119] and is informed of false matters or matters which are prepared to come in the near future.[120]

Chapter Two

On the effects of different kinds of foods.

This chapter is divided into two sections, the first on the different effects of foods according to their nature, and the second on the effects resulting from intellectual differences.

Section One

Regarding the nature of foods. The astrologers have written that we should beware of foods and drugs associated with Mars, which denotes falsehood; indulging in these foods or drugs results in false dreams. Foods associated with Mercury, Saturn, and the Sun, however, are true. Those associated with Mars are the fruits of any tree which has thorns, pears, peppers, mustard, cumin, radish, leek, garlic, rutabaga, myrrh oil[121] from myrrh[122] or sycamore resin,[123] sandalwood,[124] saffron, the skin of a hare. Those associated with Jupiter are flocks, deer, chicken, doves, nuts, almonds, peaches, hazelnuts, pistachios—any fruit with a skin or shell which must be removed so that what is inside may be eaten—wheat, barley, rice, lavender,[125] peas, musk, camphor, *piyoniya,*[126] ginger seed, raisins, cheese, aspic. Those associated with Mercury: foxes, starlings, bees—any bird that flies swiftly and any beast that runs quickly, geese, ethrog, pomegranate, all types of sap, zangwill, castor bean. Sour-tasting foods of all kinds denote Saturn: monkey, black dogs, eagle, raven, bat, mosquito, fly, mouse, gallnut, carob, crab apples, lupines, lentils. Those associated with the Sun: lion, sheep, palm, grape vine, olive, apple, berries, figs.

Section Two

According to the intellect.

Our dreams are associated with the foods we eat in yet another way. Just as coarse, bulky foods give rise to evil humors in the body, so too do they give rise to coarseness in the soul, as is known from the reason why some foods are forbidden in the laws of Kashrut. Our Sages noted that the word *ve-nitmetem,* "and you will become unclean," is written defectively[127] in order to hint that unclean foods are undesirable because they coarsen (*metamtem*) the heart.[128] Therefore, someone who eats them will certainly be unable to receive the Divine grace perfectly, unlike someone who eats refined foods. And so Pharaoh, Nebuchadnezzar, and the Cupbearer had more accurate dreams because they ate at the king's table.

This may, in fact, be what our Sages were hinting at when they stated that "all dreams follow the mouth";[129] that is to say, all dreams follow the foods which a person puts into his mouth, even though the true intent of this statement is different, as will be explained in Gate Seven, with God's help.

It would also seem to be the case that the longer the food has had to digest, the more accurate the dream. . . .

Chapter Three

Regarding differences in thought.

Bear in mind that most dreams contain images taken from the dreamer's daily activities; this sort of dream is meaningless, since it comes not from the dream master[130] but from the dreamer's imagination. In most dreams, even true ones, matters of this sort are mixed in with the essential true matter of the dream. This is proven by the Talmudic statement that a person who dreams about a married woman is assured of having a portion in the world to come[131]—so long as he had not been thinking about her during the day. Apparently the dream would be meaningless, then, if he had been thinking about her during the day.

Another Talmudic passage also proves my contention:

[The Roman emperor][132] said to R. Joshua [b. Hananya]: "You [Jews] say you are very wise; tell me what I will see in my dream." "You will see the Persians making you do forced labor, robbing you, and making you feed unclean animals with a golden staff." He thought about this all day and that night he saw it in a dream.

And so too the Talmud recounts the following incident wherein King Shapur of Persia said to Samuel,

"You say you are very wise; tell me what I will see in my dream." "You will see the Romans come and capture you, forcing you to grind datepits in a golden mill." He thought about this all day and that night saw it in a dream.[133]

It is hardly likely that these passages mean that the dreams came true because the thought had been planted in the kings' minds; how improbable! Furthermore, if this were so, anyone could think "good thoughts" during the day so as to have good dreams at night and assure a happy future for himself![134]

In conclusion, dreams which come about because of the dreamer's daytime thoughts are of no significance. . . .

[There follows a discussion of Biblical and Talmudic proofs for the contention that even true dreams contain admixtures of vain imaginings.]

It seems to me that the Talmudic Sages referred to this in the following passage: "Said R. Huna: 'A good person only has evil dreams, and an evil person only has good dreams.' We have also learned the following: 'David never in his life had a good dream, and Ahitophel never in his life had an evil dream.' But is it not written: 'No evil shall occur to you'?[135] R. Yirmiah b. Abba said:[136] 'This means that you will not be disturbed either by bad dreams or by evil thoughts.'" And they concluded that even though "he [i.e., the wicked person] does not have an evil dream, others have one about him."[137]

The explanation of this passage is that the dreams of the righteous are actually good and not evil, as R. Yirmiah asserted; R. Huna's statement that [a righteous person] only has evil dreams simply means that when he has a good dream he forgets it, and it is as if he did not have a good dream, but rather an evil one, since he wonders whether the dream he cannot remember was propitious or not. The wicked, on the other hand, only have propitious dreams.

In truth, however, the latter statement also requires explanation, since if the dreams of the wicked are always good, and those of the righteous are likewise good but are promptly forgotten, then there should be no evil dreams at all! But we know that frightening dreams occur every day. Furthermore, we know that the righteous do have good dreams and remember them, as the dreams of Joseph prove. Similarly, those of Nebuchadnezzar or Pharaoh's Chief Baker, which were evil, or the dreams of Pharaoh himself, which were both good and bad, prove [that all people, good and bad, have all sorts of dreams]. And this is the case even if we interpret the Talmudic passage as referring to *most* but not all dreams, since even then the passage will not conform to reality.

Therefore, it seems to me that the Sages, may their memory be blessed, did not really intend the statement that the righteous have frightening dreams and the wicked have joyful ones to point up a difference between the righteous and the wicked on dream interpretation, but only regarding dream images. Both the wicked and the righteous have dreams that can be interpreted both favorably and unfavorably, but there is a difference between the images by means of which the prophecy is given.

The righteous are shown good and bad dreams by means of frightening images, in conformity with the verse, "The Lord has done this in order that they fear Him,"[138] which R. Yohanan interpreted as referring to an evil dream.[139] As for the wicked, they are shown good dreams so that they will be encouraged to enjoy this world and forfeit the next, as Rashi explains there. . . .

We will understand this properly when we remember that the righteous spend their days in fear of Heaven and of Divine punishment, and thus their dreams are full of frightening images of punishment and fear. On the other hand, as was noted above, a wicked person's daytime thoughts concern pleasure because the dream itself is always a mixture of pleasing images even if its essential message is evil. Thus, Joseph's dreams were actually frightening, but as a great dream interpreter, he was able to sift the essential from the non-essential in the light of his own self-knowledge and his knowledge of his daytime thoughts. . . .

Chapter Four

Treating the effect of time on dreams.

This chapter is divided into two sections, the first on our own and ancient times, and the second, our own time.

Section One

The difference between the dreams of people on different [spiritual levels] and with different degrees of [spiritual and moral] preparation has already been explained.

And since there is no question but that the spiritual level of former generations was greater than our own, so too must there be a difference in the dreams which come to both. As is well known and almost palpable, most or all of the earlier generations were close to the Divine Presence and prepared for prophecy, but now in our times the word of the Lord is rarely encountered and vision is not widespread.[140] For this reason the dreams of earlier times were more often accurate than those of our time; most dreams in our time are more enigmatic and confusing than those of former times. Therefore, more wisdom is needed for their interpretation than was required then, and so we have been left in the dark and no one understands their intent.

Section Two

Regarding the difference in the time of the dream.

Quite clearly, the periods of a person's life are not alike [in spiritual potential]. There are times when one is more prepared for Divine Service than at other times. . . . I have found many differences related to whether the dream occurs on the first, second, or third day of the month; indeed, each day of the month is different from the others in this respect. This point was transmitted by R. Hai Gaon and the wise men who followed him, each emending it in his own way. However, it is found neither in the Talmud nor in the midrashim, and I do not know its source; perhaps it was transmitted by oral tradition from the Sinaitic revelation, or perhaps it was derived from experience.

However that may be, I have found a hint of this principle in the Torah, in the verse "We dreamed a dream that night, I and he."[141] This verse is difficult: does it make any difference whether the two dreams were dreamed on the same night or over two nights?. . . . [That is not the issue; the Chief Cupbearer simply wanted to assure Pharaoh that Joseph, as an outstanding interpreter, had been able to discern the difference between his dream and the Baker's even though they both occurred on the same night.]

I found another proof for this principle in the word of our Sages in Genesis Rabba on the verse, "'And his father [i.e., Joseph's father, Jacob] kept the matter [of Joseph's dreams] to himself.'[142] [Said R. Levi:] When Jacob heard that dream, he took pen in hand and recorded the day and hour and place."[143]

Note that Jacob was careful to note the day of the month on which Joseph dreamed the dream, the day of the week, and the time, for morning dreams are more likely to come to pass. Likewise he recorded the place, for the land of Israel is more open to Divine influence than other lands.

[A Table of Dates]

Day 1 of the Month: Whatever you dream will turn to joy.

Day 2–3: There is no truth in them [any dream on these days].

Day 4–5: Whatever you dream will come to pass only after a long time.

Day 6: Whatever you dream will come to pass, whether good or evil.

Day 7: Whatever you dream will come to pass after a while.

Day 8–9: Whatever you dream will come to pass as you dream it.

Day 10–11: Whatever you dream will come to pass after a while but without accident.

Day 12: Whatever good you dream will soon come to pass.

Day 13–14: Whatever you dream will come to pass as you dream it within eighteen days, and therefore offer prayer and supplication before your Creator, for He is forgiving and compassionate, long-suffering, and full of lovingkindness, taking back evil decrees.

Day 15–16: Whatever you dream will come to pass after a while.

Day 17: Whatever you dream will come to pass in four or five days, and afterwards you will rejoice.

Day 18–19: Whatever you dream will come to pass after a long time, but not everything that you dream.

Day 20–21: The [dreams on these days] lie; some say: if they come to pass, there will be rejoicing.

Day 22: If you rise, it will come to pass in eight days.

Day 23: Whatever you dream will be turned into argument and dispute.

Day 24: You will go out to peace and rejoicing.

Day 25–26: The dream will be fulfilled in eight or ten days, but meanwhile pray to God.

Day 27–28–29: It will turn to peace and rejoicing.

Day 30: You will be in distress, but ask mercy from God and He will have mercy on you; alternatively: If you dream about any kind of trouble, peace will come thereafter.

I have also often heard that a dream dreamed on the Sabbath will be accurate, since the "extra" soul we are given on that day leaves us more open to Divine influence.

Chapter Five

On differences in the dream's effect on the dreamer.

The most striking difference between true and untrue dreams is the effect on the dreamer. If you see the dream through powerful imaginings, so that it has an intense effect on you while you are asleep, and you feel anger and trembling pass while in the dreaming state, the dream is true; but if you see it only weakly, and are not at all emotionally affected by it, the dream is not true; everything depends on the effect. This view is supported by reason, for in the case of prophecy, the emotional impact takes place when the body's senses have been lulled to sleep, so that the powers of the mind will be strengthened and remain active. The same occurs with a dream. . . .

It further seems to me that a dream's degree of truthfulness is related to the agent causing the dream, with the most accurate dreams coming from agents on the higher levels. Prophetic dreams come from God Himself, whereas ordinary dreams from an agent much closer to the dreamer. . . .

Gate Four

Explaining the images commonly seen or not seen in dreams.

This gate is divided into three chapters. The first explores the question of whether dreams of indifferent import, neither good nor evil, are possible; the second, whether philosophical knowledge can be transmitted by dreams; and the third explains the statement of our Sages that a person is only shown the imaginings of his heart.[144]

Chapter One

Whether it is possible for matters which have
no relevance to good or bad happenings to occur.

Regarding this R. Isaac Arundi wrote in his commentary on Job, in reference to Elihu's first reply to Job,[145] that it is possible for dreams to contain matter which presages neither good nor evil, as in a dream about past events, or a dream in which someone goes to a certain place or brings something to someone else. . . .

With all due respect to the rabbi, it appears to me that his thesis was incorrect. His reference to dreaming about past events, for example, is refuted by our Sages, may their memory be blessed, who asked rhetorically in Chapter *Gid Hanasheh* in tractate Hullin of the Talmud, "Is a person ever shown what has already happened?"[146] And when he speaks of dreaming about someone going somewhere, expert dream interpreters maintain that even dreams of this kind are relevant to matters of good or evil. This will be explained after we lay out a principle to be discussed in the next gate, namely, that a dream's message is not to be found in its literal content, but rather the dreamer is shown things analogous to it, through metaphor and parable.[147] Obviously, a dream interpreter must interpret a dream that utilizes metaphor or parable in the light of positive or negative outcomes. This will become clearer as the purpose of this form of communication is revealed.

The preceding point resembles what R. Levi ben Gershon writes in his *Wars of the Lord*.[148] He attributes the existence of dreams to Providence.

Humans have been created as creatures possessing free will, and therefore able to seek good and distance themselves from evil, but they are vulnerable to whatever Fate[149] has in store for them, unable to discern whether what happens betokens good or evil. For this reason, the kind of knowledge obtained through dreams was granted them in order that they might be saved from what was in store for them, whether by their own efforts on the material plane or through repentance and good deeds, prayer and supplication before God that He might abolish the evil decree. Similarly, humankind is also given foreknowledge in regard to favorable events, in order to hasten their realization. . . . [150] [R. Almoli proceeds to show how Gersonides' rule is borne out by the various Biblical dreams which have already been discussed; all worked to the benefit of the righteous or the detriment of the wicked, and helped to further God's plan.]

In truth, what we have said means that when someone is told what is going to happen to him, this communication takes place so as to motivate him to try to annul the evil if he can. And when he is informed of some good thing that is going happen to him, the communication is intended to induce him to aid in its realization. Possibly, and perhaps even probably, the dreamer will not do what is required in the wake of his dreams, and in consequence the good will be annulled and the evil come to pass; this results from a lack on the part of the dreamer, who either did not understand the dream or did not take the action needed to avert the evil or encourage the good. . . .

As for encouraging the fulfillment of a favorable omen, there is a proof from the Zohar, regarding "And Joseph remembered the dreams he had dreamed."[151]

Come and see: A dream which is not interpreted is like a letter which is not read;[152] note that if it is not remembered, [the dreamer] has no knowledge of it. One whose dream is forgotten does not know to [attempt to] fulfill it; thus he must remember his dream in order to fulfill it. . . . [153]

Thus, they said explicitly that one must remember a good dream in order to try to help in its fulfillment, for if the dream is forgotten, one will be unable to do this, and the dream will be like a letter that is not read—useless. . . .

Chapter Two

Whether dreams can provide information regarding
theoretical aspects of the various sciences or not.

Gersonides, may his memory be blessed, investigated this in his *Wars of the Lord,* and presented two compelling arguments which assert that it is impossible to attain understanding of metaphysical speculations without having mastered their underlying premises, as would be the case with information derived from a dream.

First, if this were so, it would be equivalent to God's knowledge, and should thus be called "thought" and not "knowledge," for true knowledge as we define it is impossible without the premises which bring it forth. Since knowledge obtained by this means of communication [i.e., dreams] would by definition be incorrect [because its premises would be lacking,] it is not [to be defined as true knowledge] and there is no use in attempting to obtain it.

Furthermore, if it were possible to attain knowledge of such matters without their premises, there would be no need for the senses in the acquisition of axioms, and the use of logical proofs would also be unnecessary—these are his words, may his memory be blessed.[154]

[R. Almoli now presents the arguments of Ibn Rushd (Averroes)[155] on the same theme, countering them with various accounts, some from Gersonides, of medical and philosophical knowledge imparted by dreams. He continues with a number of similar incidents recorded in the Talmud and by later authorities regarding matters of Torah knowledge.]

Chapter "These Are Burnt" of tractate Sanhedrin 82a gives an account of a query which R. Kahana made of Rav, regarding a man who has intercourse with a gentile woman. [The Mishnah lays down the rule that he is to be dealt with by zealots; R. Kahana] asked what the law is in a case in which they do not deal with him [i.e., what is his punishment?]. Rav completely forgot the law in this case. The following verse was read to R. Kahana in a dream: "Judah has been unfaithful and an abomination has been done in Israel and in Jerusalem, for Judah has profaned what is holy to God, what He loves, and has had relations with the daughter of an alien god."[156] He [i.e., R. Kahana] said to him [i.e.,

35

Rav]: Thus it had been recited before me in a dream, and Rav remembered his tradition. . . .

And who is greater for us than R. Moses bar Yaakov, author of *Sefer Mitzvot Gadol,* may his memory be blessed, who testified that he was shown a speculative matter in a dream, namely, that the verse "Take care lest you forget the Lord your God"[157] is to be counted as a prohibition of the 613 commandments, just the contrary of the position taken by other Sages on the matter? . . . This is also true in the area of prophecy, where we find that myriads of ideas have come to dreamers who had no prior knowledge of the axioms upon which these ideas were based, such as the visions of Ezekiel and Isaiah of the Divine Chariot.[158]

[R. Almoli now presents the classic argument, going back to R. Saadiah Gaon, on the necessity of two modes of attaining knowledge: the philosophical method of axiom and proof for the educated elite, and revelation for all those, including the elite, who cannot fathom every aspect of metaphysics without the help of Divine revelation. Dreams are naturally part of the latter method. However, knowledge attained by revelatory means is superior in that it is not subject to doubt.]

I have not adopted Gersonides' answer to these questions with which the chapter began, for anyone who analyzes his arguments on this subject will be left with many doubts; there is no need to continue with a lengthy exposition here.

In conclusion, while some understanding of philosophical questions may be obtained by means of dreams, this really happens only to a small extent and infrequently . . . and only in areas where it is difficult for the unaided human mind to obtain understanding, so that if one was not informed of them, he would remain in a state of incurable blindness. Divine Providence, in a dream or a prophecy, informs him of these matters in a manner more easily assimilated.

Chapter Three

Regarding that which our Sages, may their memory be blessed, stated: "A person is shown in dreams only the imaginings of his heart."[159]

We read in Chapter "He Who Sees":

Said R. Samuel b. Nahmani in the name of R. Yonatan: "A person is shown only the imaginings of his heart, as it is said, 'As for you, O King, your thoughts came into your mind on your bed' [Daniel 2:29], or if you wish, [I can prove this from the following verse,] 'that you may know the thoughts of your heart' [ibid., 2:30]." Said Rava: "This is proved by the fact that a person is never shown in a dream a date palm of gold or an elephant going through the eye of a needle."[160]

There is a question as to which of the two interpretations of this passage is correct. Does it mean that a person only dreams about things he is concerned with, in order to rid him of his perplexity regarding them, even though it would be possible to inform him of these things by means of metaphor and parable, which can happen while he is awake? Or does it mean that he is informed of things that Heaven wishes to inform him about, but not by means of strange metaphors and parables that cannot possibly occur while he is awake, but by employing metaphors and parables with which his mind is occupied while awake? In essence, the question is whether this passage[161] refers to the dream itself or to its interpretation.

Both interpretations of the passage are possible; the first proof from the verse supports the first interpretation, for the dream referred to there dealt with future events of which Nebuchadnezzar wished to have knowledge, as the verse states, "As for you, O King, your thoughts which came into your mind on your bed are about future events; He who reveals mysteries has let you know what is about to happen" [Daniel 2:29], and therefore it would seem that the correct interpretation of this Talmudic passage is that a person is given knowledge only of matters with which he occupies himself when awake.

But regarding Rava's proof from experience, that a person never dreams about a golden date palm or an elephant going through the eye of a needle, it would seem that a person is informed of future events only by means of metaphors and parables which involve matters or objects with which he is occupied when awake, and not matters which cannot occur, viz., a golden date palm or an elephant going through the eye of a needle. . . .

The second interpretation seems to be correct in light of the anecdote recorded above in Gate Three, Chapter Three, regarding R. Joshua b. Hananiah and the Roman emperor.

> [The Roman emperor][162] said to R. Joshua [b. Hanania]: "You [Jews] say you are very wise; tell me what I will see in my dream." "You will see the Persians making you do forced labor, robbing you, and making you feed unclean animals with a golden staff." He thought about this all day and at night he saw it in a dream.

And so too [the Talmud recounts the following incident wherein] King Shapur [of Persia] said to Samuel,

> "You say you are very wise; tell me what I will see in my dream." "You will see the Romans come and capture you, forcing you to grind date-pits in a golden mill." He thought about this all day and in the night saw it in a dream.[163]

This makes it clear that one only dreams about things he may think about during the day. Rashi explains the passage the same way, for he notes that a person is shown only that which he thinks about during the day, and therefore is not shown a golden palm, for this is something which people *do not customarily see, and therefore never think about.* This being so, the verses which are cited in opposition are to be regarded simply as "pegs" on which to hang R. Samuel b. Nahmani's statement, and not as absolute proofs.

However, this interpretation is bitter to me in light of the objection which I analyzed above, in Gate Three, Chapter Three.[164] Therefore I have reconsidered my position, and now assert that both meanings are implicit in this Talmudic passage. A person dreams only about things that concern him, and is informed of these things only by parables meaningful to him in terms of his daily activities.

In general, therefore, the principle that a person is only shown things with which he is occupied applies to both the subject of the dream and the metaphors employed therein. . . .

As for the second part of the passage, however, I must explain that its intent is not to say that what a person thinks during the day and then occurs in a dream at night is necessarily true, for we have proven the contrary in the chapter mentioned above. Rather, our Sages, may their memory be blessed, sought to show us the nature and pattern of dreams, namely, that whatever a person is shown in a dream, in the form of metaphors or parables representing the knowledge to be imparted to him, always comes from things that can actually happen and conform to reality, regarding which his mind is occupied during the day. . . .

Further proof of this is the fact that people often dream about things which they did *not* think about during the day, but hardly ever about things that are impossible of occurrence while awake. However, if a person does dream about something strange that cannot occur in reality—this is seldom the case. It happens because sometimes a person burdens his mind with bizarre matters high and low, and since his thoughts are only seldom occupied with such things, they make a greater impression and he dreams about them.

R. Shemtov ibn Shemtov,[165] may his memory be blessed, interpreted the passage in Midrash Tanhuma in this manner:

May our masters teach us: What is the difference between the dreams of the righteous and the dreams of the wicked? The dreams of the righteous are of the heavens and of the earth, the dreams of the wicked are neither of the heavens nor of the earth.

Jacob's dream was of the earth, as it is stated, "And behold a ladder was set on the earth";[166] his dream was of the heavens, as it is stated, "And its top reached the heavens."[167]

Joseph's dreams were of the earth, as it is stated, "There we were binding sheaves in the field";[168] his dreams were of the heavens, as it is stated, "The sun, the moon, and eleven stars."[169]

Pharaoh's dreams, however, were neither of the heavens nor of the earth, as it is stated, "Behold, I was standing near the river."[170]

This hints, he says, at the great difference between the dreams of the righteous and of the wicked, which resembles the difference between the two when awake. A righteous person desires knowledge of Divine matters and of all of reality in its proper ordering, how its causes and effects are intertwined as they issue from the heavenly sphere and from the First Cause, the Cause of All Causes [i.e., God], after which they [the righteous] seek to learn how to perfect humankind, those earthbound creatures. Therefore, the dreams of the righteous are like their actions while awake; they concern matters both of heaven and of earth, as illustrated by Jacob and Joseph. However, the wicked, whose waking actions are not accomplished with spiritual or bodily perfection, do not dream of these matters.

Gate Five

Explaining three essential principles which a dream interpreter must
understand if his interpretations are to be correct, for these indicate
the nature of each dream.

This gate is divided into two chapters: Chapter One, setting forth the three
essential principles, and Chapter Two, applying them to Joseph's interpretations
of Pharaoh's dreams.

Chapter One

(1) When a dream recurs two or three times in the same form,[171] it is
sometimes intended to indicate the dream's veracity or to clarify [certain details
which were unclear the first time], even though [all of the dreams] refer to the
same interpretation or incident. At other times, the recurrences each refer to
separate incidents that will all occur in the future.

How do we determine which of these two purposes is behind the
repetition of the dream?

If the repetitions recur in exactly the same fashion, without any change, even
though the symbolism shifts, then even if the dream is repeated a hundred times, it
refers to the same incident. . . . If however the repetition differs [in that it provides
more details], then aside from the purpose of stressing the veracity [of the first
occurrence of the dream], it comes to clarify additional details. . . .

If however there are substantive changes in the repetition, it should be
interpreted in as many different ways as there are repetitions. . . .

The first contention is proven by Pharaoh's two dreams, both of which
referred to seven years of plenty and seven of famine. The proof of the second
is that Joseph's two dreams regarding the sheaves and stars differed in the
number of persons bowing down to him, thus referring to two separate
incidents.

[Here follows a detailed interpretation of the differences between Joseph's two dreams, and their significance].

The second essential principle is the one that Aristotle wrote about in his book, *De sensu et sensato*: the subject matter of dreams does not issue from the dreamer but rather from matters close to him in body and soul, or to his relatives or fellow citizens of his city or his people—that is, from what is generally known and what people think about or imagine, but not dreams which concern the world in general as will be explained.

Our Sages agree with this principle, but add the proviso that kings and nobles have dreams which concern the world in general. They stated this in Genesis Rabba:

"And Pharaoh dreamed."[172] Do not all people dream? [Why say particularly that Pharaoh dreamed?] However, a monarch's dream involves matters concerning the whole world.[173]

They are saying here that while we all dream about things that pertain to us as individuals, a king's dreams pertain to the entire world. . . . Similarly, the Zohar says:

Even though it has been stated that dreams are shown to a person only in regard to his own thought, kings are different in that they have dreams about supernal matters which are different from those shown other people, in that a king's degree is higher than that of other people, as Scripture states: "What God is about to do He has shown Pharaoh."[174] However, the Holy One, blessed be He, does not reveal to other people what He is about to do, except to the prophets or the pious or to the wise men of the generation. . . . [175]

This principle is proven by the dreams of Joseph and Pharaoh's officials,[176] which concerned things relevant only to them, while the dreams of Nebuchadnezzar involved matters of more general import. . . .

The third principle holds that matters revealed in a dream are not shown in the precise form in which they will occur, but symbolically or metaphorically. This is similar to the form of prophecy, as is well known. All the dreams in Scripture and in the writings of our Sages demonstrate the truth of this principle.

[Chapter Two interprets Pharaoh's dreams in exquisitely fine detail.]

Gate Six

Explaining that every interpretation should follow
the dreamer's work and interests.

As the wise know, while two persons may have the same dream, the interpreter must apply his knowledge of the dreamers and not interpret the dreams identically. For example, a horse may represent either wisdom or strength. Thus, if a wise man dreams that he manages with great difficulty to cross a river while riding a horse, this indicates that he will overcome great obstacles by using his wisdom. However, if the dreamer is not a wise man but a strong and valiant one, we should interpret the horse as representing strength rather than wisdom. Likewise; if a highway robber dreams he is being hanged from a palm, the interpretation will not be the same as it would be for a young scholar who dreamed the same thing, for each interpretation follows the situation of the dreamer; in one case the dreamer will be hanged, in the other rulership is indicated, as is explained at the end of tractate Yoma.

Rabbi Hanina dreamed that Rav was being hanged from a palm in Babylon. Now, tradition has it that one who is hanged on a palm will become a leader; thus he concluded that Rav would become a head [of a yeshiva and therefore sent him to Babylon to establish a yeshiva there].[177]

This principle is hidden from fools who claim knowledge of this science of dream interpretation but really know nothing about it. . . .

Gate Seven

An analysis concerning a topic of great utility explaining whether dreams follow their interpretation or not; it is divided into three chapters.

Chapter One contains the essential analysis; Two, an explanation of three axioms which require elaboration; Three, regarding the interpretation of dreams.

Chapter One

We find in Chapter "One Who Sees" of the Talmud tractate Berakhot, chap. 9: "A dream which is not interpreted is like a letter which is not read."[178] This means that if a dream is not interpreted—for instance, when someone is silent and does not reveal his dream (so that it cannot be interpreted)—it is as if the dream were never dreamed; it will not be fulfilled in any way, neither for good nor for ill, just as when a letter arrives from far off and sits unopened and unread. [An unread letter] is as if it had not been sent, for the recipient has no knowledge of what is written in it. It has also been stated that "All dreams follow the mouth," which is most often explained as meaning that the interpretation of a dream affects its fulfillment, as Scripture states, "As he interpreted it for us, so did it come to pass."[179] Put differently, if a dream denotes evil, but is given a favorable interpretation, it will follow the favorable interpretation, and if the reverse, so too.

This is so much the case that the Sages stated in the Talmud that:

R. Bizna b. Zavda said in the name of R. Akiva, who had it in the name of R. Parnakh, again in the name of R. Nahum in the name of R. Biram, who had it from an old man, and who was that? R. Nehorai: There were twenty-four interpreters of dreams in Jerusalem; once I dreamed a dream and went to each of them, and each gave [the dream] a different interpretation—"but all [the interpretations] were fulfilled in my life. This illustrates what is said: All dreams follow the mouth" [i.e., the interpretation].[180]

According to these axioms, however, we must ask why the dream interpretations recorded in the Talmud and in other books as to when they would be fulfilled were written. For there are two possibilities: Either the dreamer remained silent and did not tell anyone his dream, in which case it was not interpreted for him, or he told it and it was interpreted for him. If he did not report the dream, [then we know, following the first axiom,] that it was as though it had never been dreamed [and so why record the incident?]. [On the other hand,] if it had been interpreted, [we understand, in accordance with the second axiom,] that its fulfillment follows its interpretation, and not the interpretation recorded in the book. Then why did the Sages of the Talmud or the writer of the book bother to record their own interpretations, since the dream follows the interpretation given [to the dreamer at the time of his inquiry, and not that recorded in books; there are no standard interpretations].

Apparently these interpretations would have come to pass even if the dreamer had remained silent but opened a book of dream interpretations and read the meaning of his dream. In this case, the interpretation was accomplished by his seeing it in a book; what is the difference between an interpretation given by another person and one seen in a book? In the end, after all, an interpretation is an interpretation!

According to this, if he had not seen the book's interpretation, but instead went and reported the dream to someone who then explained it, whether positively or negatively, the dream would have followed the interpretation given and not that in the book. However, if after this he had read the book's interpretation, that too would have come to pass, as the Talmud recorded regarding the twenty-four dream interpreters in Jerusalem, etc.[181] If, however, he dreams of something which is not explained in a book, the dream will never be fulfilled until someone interprets it for the dreamer.

This answer is not without merit, but upon further reflection it is wrong, for if it were correct, the Sages should only have given positive interpretations, and a person seeking an interpretation would only have to open a book in order to obtain rest for his soul, and all dreams would be positive. If so, the question recurs.

Furthermore, if all dreams follow the mouth, and a person given a favorable interpretation can cancel the interpretation found in books, then any fool can set himself up as a dream interpreter, and no wisdom is needed for it. This is surely not so, for there is certainly much wisdom involved in dream interpretation, as Pharaoh said to Joseph: "Since the Lord has informed you of all this, there is no one as understanding and wise as you."[182] Similarly, in the case of Daniel, Scripture testifies to his superior wisdom, in that he had a better understanding of dream interpretation than they, as it is said: "As for these four lads, the Lord gave them intelligence and proficiency in all writings and wisdom, and Daniel had understanding of visions and dreams of all kinds."[183] Scripture's hint regarding this point has already been explained in the Introduction. . . . Since explaining dreams depends on wisdom, it cannot be the case that anyone who wants to acquire a reputation as a dream interpreter can do so; rather it is a rare ability, "one from a city and two from a tribe."[184] Note what Joseph himself said: "Are not interpretations the Lord's?" and "The Lord will give Pharaoh an answer of peace."[185] What we may understand from his words is that the interpretation of dreams is a Divine matter, and a true understanding of it cannot be achieved without Divine inspiration.

The expression "follows the mouth" apparently means just the opposite of the general understanding, to wit, that any interpreter, whoever he may be, [can determine the fulfillment of the dream].

I find this quite difficult to accept. Are we to understand that whatever the Lord wishes to do He announces[186] to anyone He wishes, showing him what is about to happen by means of a visionary dream whose meaning is nullified if it is not interpreted, [thus defeating God's purpose,] and changes so as to follow the interpreter's interpretation if it is interpreted, [again defeating God's purpose]?

The explanation given in Genesis Rabba for the verse "there was no one to interpret it for Pharaoh"[187] is also difficult. [This is how the Sages cited in Genesis Rabba understand the verse:] "Interpreters there were, but not for Pharaoh. For they would say to him: Seven daughters will you beget and seven daughters will you bury; seven provinces will you conquer and seven provinces will rebel against you."[188] But we find that these interpretations were not fulfilled, since they were not true. Likewise, oftentimes a person has his dreams interpreted but they are not fulfilled in accordance with the interpretations. We cannot say that these dreams are null and void and have no true interpretation, because we have already proven that there is no such thing as a dream without an interpretation.[189]

In consequence, we must ascertain the meaning of "all dreams follow the mouth." We must also understand how a dream can be explained in several contradictory ways; if dream interpretation is a science, what one interpreter knows all should know.

The Tosafists[190] evidently tried to solve this problem in their comment on the Talmud text regarding the twenty-four dream interpreters.

It seems to R. Isaac [of Dampierre] that the constellation [in the ascendant] at the birth [of the interpreter] causes the interpretation [to be fulfilled]; the matter does not depend on wisdom.[191]

But to my way of thinking, this proposal does not suffice to answer the question raised, since in our time "vision is infrequent and vision is uninterpreted,"[192] and I have found no dream interpreter whose interpretations will [inevitably] be fulfilled. If everything depended on astrological signs, we should be able to find someone to explicate dreams even in our own times, as in ancient times, since the heavenly spheres rotate and return to the same place year after year. Moreover, how could there be so many dream interpreters residing in the same city with astrological signs that enabled their interpretations to be fulfilled, and not one with an evil sign, while in our own time there are very few whose signs are not evil? Furthermore, as we have already proven, it all depends on great wisdom and not on astrology.

Chapter Two

Explaining the axioms needed to resolve the problem
raised in Chapter One.

The first axiom is that the rules governing dream interpretation must be based on a prior detailed knowledge of the dreamer's private life. From this and its implications the interpreter, to the extent of his intellectual ability, will assess future events. This is appropriate for those who are able to provide advice to enlighten the eyes of knaves and fools, that is, those who have the power to assess circumstances as the *Guide* [i.e., Maimonides] wrote in II:35 of the *Guide of the Perplexed*. [R. Almoli proceeds to provide two Biblical examples of such individuals, Ahitophel and Samuel, quoting Narboni on the *Guide* in the process.]

Now, the person who has these powers can take into consideration, to the extent his knowledge permits, the many factors pertaining to the dreamer's prior and changing situation, and can produce a true explanation of the implications of the dream. He must also be able to comprehend parabolic and symbolic language, the words and riddles of the wise, in order truly to understand the dream's implications.

It is apparent that the powers of assessment of Joseph the Righteous were strengthened by his acuity in matters pertaining to the acquisition of wealth and in knowledge of which merchandise would rise in price and which would fall, regarding which King Solomon, may his memory be blessed, said, "The hand of the diligent makes rich."[193] Potiphar and his wife observed Joseph's great success in all his undertakings, whether at home or in the field. His superiority in the art of assessing future possibilities is also evident in the advice he gave to Pharaoh regarding the grain, whereby Pharaoh acquired all the wealth of the entire land of Egypt. With this power, too, Joseph accurately interpreted the dreams of Pharaoh's officials, which could easily have both been interpreted the same way rather than differently, for Scripture says: "And they dreamed a dream, both of them."[194] Joseph nevertheless gave them separate interpretations based on what he knew of them from having spent time with them in prison, as well as on what he knew of the differences between their professions and in their relative closeness to the king. [R. Almoli goes on to enumerate the various fine details of the dreams whose significance Joseph correctly explained.]

Thus, Joseph recognized the differences between the two dreams by means of his knowledge of previous circumstances, and this applies also to every wise man who interprets dreams accurately.

In Chapter "He Who Sees" [i.e., tractate Berakhot, chapter 9, the so-called "Tractate on Dreams"]: "A certain person came to R. Yose b. Halafta and said to him: 'It was said to me in a dream: "Go fetch your father's bailment from Cappadocia."' 'Was your father ever in Cappadocia?' the latter asked. 'No.' "If so, count to the tenth beam of your house and there you will find it.' 'I don't have ten beams in my house.' 'In that case, count from beginning to end and back, and there you will find it.' He went, did so, and found it full of gold coins."[195] A similar story is recorded in Genesis Rabba, as mentioned above in Gate One, Chapter Three.[196] [From this R. Almoli infers that knowledge of previous circumstances aids in the accurate interpretation of dreams, and he cites other stories in the same vein from Eicha Rabba.]

The second axiom is that every dream contains many different denotations, both negative and positive, on a range of matters. This is what Joseph alluded to when he said to Pharaoh: "Are not interpretations the Lord's?" He intentionally used the plural, "interpretations," for he was explaining the dreams both for his own and for future generations. [R. Almoli cites other proofs for this contention.]

The third axiom is that it is almost impossible for a man of great wisdom to interpret dreams accurately in accordance with their proper meaning, because error is unavoidable. For this reason one should not rely on oneself in interpreting dreams but should go to an expert who has studied the subject, and be guided by him, as I have discussed in the Introduction to this book.

Chapter Three

After all this it should now be evident that our Sages' statement that "all dreams follow the mouth" does not mean that an interpreter can nullify the implications of a dream by giving an interpretation that opposes the dream's true meaning. Rather, this statement can be explained in one of the following three ways, each based on one of the axioms examined above:

The first interpretation proceeds from the first axiom: that the interpretation of dreams follows the inquiries of the one who makes the request,[197] that he should make his affairs known so that an accurate interpretation may be made, in keeping with the interpreter's imaginative faculty. Accordingly, "mouth" here has the same sense as in the verse "Who placed a mouth [in man]"[198] [i.e., who gave man the power of speech, and likewise, the power of imagination and empathy]. Thus, each interpreter recognizes some feature of the inquirer's affairs not recognized the others, and so each interprets a different part of the dream.

The second interpretation is as follows: Every dream has several implications, as noted, and no one, no matter how well versed in this science, can understand them all. Instead, he will understand and interpret one or two, and leave the rest. The dreamer will only take note of the interpretations he has been given, and when they come to pass, he will recognize that those parts of his dream have been fulfilled, but he will not recognize the fulfillment of those parts of the dream which have *not* been interpreted. [Thus, the recognition of the fulfillment of dreams follows the "mouth," and only those interpretations will be recognizably fulfilled.] . . . It may be that this is what our Sages intended when they stated that "there is no dream without vain things interspersed";[199] by "vain things" is meant the uninterpreted parts of the dream whose fulfillment is not recognized. . . . So too the matter of the twenty-four dream interpreters in Jerusalem, each of whom recognized one specific implication of the dream.

The third interpretation of the rabbinic statement that "all dreams follow the mouth" proceeds from the third axiom, "Do not be wise in your own eyes, do not rely on your own understanding"[200] to interpret your own dreams according to whatever occurs to you. Know that a dream can bring awareness only after it has been interpreted; otherwise the dream is meaningless and as though it had not been dreamed. As our Sages said: "Every dream which is not interpreted [is like a letter which is not read]"[201] and "All dreams follow their interpretation."[202] When someone is informed of something through a dream, it is with the understanding that it will be interpreted in a specific fashion. Thus you have three interpretations of this statement, each correct and not subject to the difficulties discussed above.

This also clarifies the statement that "a dream that is not interpreted is like a letter that is not read."[203] The meaning is not that it will not be fulfilled, but that it will be fulfilled but the dreamer will be unaware of it.

So too in the Zohar:

R. Hiyya and R. Yose were often before R. Shimon. They asked him: "Regarding that which we learnt: 'A dream that is not interpreted is like a letter that is not read.' Does this mean that the dream is fulfilled without the dreamer being aware of it, or does it mean that it remains altogether unfulfilled?" He answered them: "It is fulfilled, but the dreamer is unaware of it."[204]

This can also be understood from the analogy of a dream to a letter that is not read. Just as a letter arriving from a distant place was sent to notify the recipient of something which betokens either harm or benefit to him, but if he does not open it, or even if he reads it and fails to understand it, he cannot guard himself against the harm. . . . But there is no doubt that the letter will be fulfilled despite the [recipient's failure to understand it].

In the light of all the preceding points, we are able to understand what our Sages recorded in the Midrash: "Said R. Yohanan: 'All dreams follow the interpretation except those involving the drinking of wine, for there are some who drink it and it is good for them, and some who drink it and it disagrees with them. It is good for a scholar, and bad for an ignoramus.'"[205]

Now this seems self-contradictory. First he says that dreams about wine do not follow their interpretation, and then he gives the interpretation! And if you reply that it means that the interpreter has the power to alter the import of dreams in all cases except those involving wine, then I will ask: Why are dreams involving wine different from other dreams? Moreover, there are many such dreams in Chapter "He Who Sees" [i.e., tractate Berakhot, chapter 9, the so-called "Tractate on Dreams,"] in which [minor variations lead to major differences in interpretation.] "Whoever sees a cat in a dream, if in a place where they call it a *shunara*, a beautiful song[206] will be composed for him; if in a place where they call it a *shinra*, he will undergo a change for the worse."[207] [R. Almoli gives several other, similar examples.] And no one objects that these do not follow their interpretations; indeed, it is stated that all dreams follow the interpretation. To the contrary, we must say that the intention of R. Yohanan's statement must be along the lines of the three interpretations we have already given. First: While in general it is necessary to ask the dream inquirer about his affairs and then interpret his dream, in this case it is only necessary to determine whether he is a scholar or an ignoramus, and this alone suffices for a proper interpretation, whether favorable or unfavorable. And so too according to the second of our interpretations above: All dreams have many implications and interpretations, so that what they reveal follows their interpretations, except dreams involving wine; these have only one implication, which is that if the dreamer is a scholar, etc. Finally, according to the third interpretation suggested above—that every dream requires an expert interpreter—dreams involving wine do not require expert interpretation, except if the dreamer is a scholar, etc.

In conclusion, we learn from the words of our Sages that "all dreams follow their interpretation" does not mean that interpreters are free to alter the meaning of dreams as they wish, but that each interpreter must interpret the dream presented to him according to its true import, and not what may occur to him. . . .

That is why the interpretations of Pharaoh's dreams provided by his sorcerers were not fulfilled. And so wrote Gersonides [in his commentary on the Torah], at the end of his comments on Vayeshev and the beginning of Mikketz, in the fifth Lesson: that the interpreter does not have the power to alter the import of a dream as he wishes. So too Ibn Ezra.[208]

Further proof for this contention may be found in the Talmudic passage which states: "[R. Huna b. Ammi said in the name of R. Pedat in the name of R. Yohanan]: 'If one has a dream which makes him sad, he should go and have it interpreted in the presence of three.' But has not R. Hisda said: 'A dream which is not interpreted is like a letter which is not read?' Say rather: 'He should have it "sweetened"[209] in the presence of three.'"[210] If the interpreter has the power to alter the dream, what question is being asked in R. Hisda's name? Isn't it better to have it reinterpreted from bad to good, since the interpreter has this power, than not to have it interpreted in any way, good or bad? Furthermore, what is the meaning of the answer given, that he should go and have it "sweetened" in the presence of three? Why does it need sweetening if it has not been interpreted, since after all, a dream which is not interpreted is meaningless and has no power, and so need not be sweetened?

No, the truth is as I have stated: a dream will be fulfilled even if the interpreter remains silent. From this standpoint, the passage may easily be understood. The question asked means that since the interpreter does not have the power to alter the meaning of the dream, what is the point of having it interpreted, since an evil dream will come to pass in any case; let him rather be silent! In that way the dreamer will at least avoid the evil of worrying about a future calamity. Thus the final answer given in this passage is to let the dreamer go and have the dream "sweetened"; in short, to beg mercy and pray to God, for He alone can change the decree, and no one else. . . . [R. Almoli here points out that the same may be said of Biblical dreams that seem to be beyond the power of the interpreter; for example,] why did Joseph's brothers not reinterpret his dreams of sheaves and stars in a way favorable to themselves, if that was possible? In reality, the true import of this story is that they could not prevent the fulfillment of Joseph's dream by reinterpreting it.

Similarly, the interpretations of dreams mentioned in the Talmud and in various books must be arrived at in the same manner, with the interpreter understanding all the private details of the dream in order to interpret it in accord with his judgment and intuition, in light of everything discussed in the previous gates . . .

The stories about Bar Hadaya and Rava and Abaye were recorded because of his erudition and great knowledge in the science of interpretation.[211] That is why the Talmud prefaced them with the statement that Bar Hadaya was a dream interpreter; apparently this was his profession, and he was aware of all the implications of any dream as well as the specifics of his clients' affairs. Therefore, when a dreamer paid his fee, he would give him a good reading and ignore the other negative implications. But he would do the reverse with anyone who did not pay him, interpreting the negative aspects of the dream and ignoring the positive. This strategy increased his income, because prospective clients thought that the interpretation depended on the amount of the fee. Add to this the fact that he recognized that Rava's stellar configuration was bad. Since it was Rava who had stated that "length of life, children, and sustenance do not depend on merit but on one's stellar configuration,"[212] Bar Hadaya thought that Rava's own luck was bad. For these reasons, he consistently interpreted Rava's dream negatively. His interpretation of Rava's dream was based on this view: "'The letter *vav* of the expression *peter hamor* ["the firstborn of a donkey"][213] has been erased from your tefillin.'[214]Rava examined them, and found that the letter was missing."[215]It cannot be said that this happened because of the interpretation. Furthermore, Bar Hadaya could not have interpreted a dream in this way for Abaye [Rava's colleague and rival], even if Abaye failed to pay his fee, for this circumstance pertaining to a defective letter did not apply to Abaye's tefillin; an interpreter is not a magician. This being the case, and Bar Hadaya being compelled to derive his interpretation from the actual facts of the case, why was Rava so angry at him for his negative interpretation? And why did Bar Hadaya consider himself guilty of a sin, and fear Rava's curse?

Rava, so it would seem, was not acquainted with the science of dream interpretation at that time, and that is why he resorted to Bar Hadaya for his services. Unaware of Bar Hadaya's strategy for increasing his income, he thought that Bar Hadaya could only interpret dreams according to their true significance and did not know that "all dreams follow their interpretation." When he saw [this statement in Bar Hadaya's hidden book of dream interpretation], he understood it in its plain sense,[216] and became very angry, since Bar Hadaya had not wanted to reveal this important principle to him. Rava was angered still more because Bar Hadaya could have interpreted his dreams in a less frightening way, and could have helped him to avoid their worst effects, as Daniel did for Nebuchadnezzar, saying: "My lord, would that the dream were for your enemy, and its meaning for your foe!"[217] and "Redeem your sins with charity."[218] But Bar Hadaya did not do so, instead treating Rava as an enemy merely because he had not paid his fee until he had been afflicted with great suffering. We know that this is so because he said to Rava: "I afflicted him." Consequently it would seem to have been the pain alone that caused him to curse Bar Hadaya, and that was why Bar Hadaya punished himself with exile.

[R. Almoli now cites and analyzes a similar story from Genesis Rabba 8:8.]

Because of all this, I say that the proper course of action for an interpreter, when a person comes to have a dream explained, is to give the truth as he sees it. If the interpretation is unfavorable, let him advise the dreamer to try to distance himself from it and seek God's mercy; if favorable, he should encourage the dreamer to aid in its fulfillment.

This principle, which I have arrived at after deep consideration, agrees with the comments of R. Isaac Arama[219] in Gate 29 of his *Akedat Yitzhak*; however, subsequently I found a passage in the Zohar which does not agree with him; on the contrary, it seems to disagree.

"And Joseph dreamed a dream, and told it to his brothers, and they hated him still more."[220] From this we learn that a person does not need to tell a dream to anyone but his friend, and if not, he causes evil for himself, for if the dream is altered, it is he himself who has caused [its fulfillment] to desist. Come and see that Joseph was the one who told his dreams to his brothers, and for this they caused his dream['s fulfillment] to be delayed twenty-two years.

R. Yose said: How do we know this? Because it is written, "they hated him still more." What is "hated him"? They caused heavenly charges to be levied against him in this connection. What is written [further on] "He said to them: 'Please listen to the dream which I have dreamt'"—he asked them to listen to him, and he then told them the dream, which, but for their altering its meaning, would have been fulfilled in its proper time. They replied to him,

"Will you reign over us, will you rule over us?" They then interpreted the
dream for him and made a decree, and as a result, the fulfillment of the dream
was delayed for twenty-two years.[221]

From this, it would seem, there is no alternative but to say that an
interpreter, if he so wishes, can change a dream's outcome from what he knows
to be its true meaning. And the Talmud passage and midrashim which he cites
lead to the same conclusion; and certainly there is proof from the verse "As he
interpreted, so it was,"[222] which implies that if he had interpreted the dreams
differently, that is how they would have been fulfilled, and all this is in
contradiction to our conclusions above.

However, upon further reflection the essence of the Zohar's statement
confirms everything we have said, if we understand it correctly in light of the
providential purpose of dreams.

Remember what is clear: if a dreamer has a dream intended to reveal the
good fortune in store for him, but goes to an enemy to have it interpreted, the
enemy will very probably give the dream a negative interpretation. Since the
dreamer, as a result, will be unaware of the good in store for him, he will not
try to bring it about; moreover, misguided by his enemy's false interpretation
and thinking it true, he will try to delay the fulfillment of the dream. While his
efforts to delay the dream's fulfillment will be in vain, this is still a serious defect.

However, if he goes to a friend to have the dream interpreted, whether for
good or ill, in order to speed the fulfillment of the good or delay the evil
consequences, it is clear that his friend will interpret truthfully, and it is for this
reason that the Zohar suggests that one consult with a friendly interpreter. . .
. [R. Almoli now applies this principle to Joseph. Since his brothers did not
want the dreams of his rulership fulfilled, they scoffed at them, and he, believing
what they said, did nothing to help the dreams come about. As a result, their
fulfillment was delayed by twenty-two years.]

Moreover, I found a similar interpretation in the Torah commentary of R.
Yose Ibn Nahamias,[223] *parashat* Vayeshev, in the name of R. Yaakov son of
Asheri.[224] He asks why Joseph's dreams were not nullified by the brothers'
scoffing and his father's reproof, since "all dreams follow their interpretation."
His solution to this problem is that the long delay in the dreams' fulfillment was
tantamount to nullification, for had Jacob not reproved Joseph for them, they
would quickly have been fulfilled. . . .

Gate Eight

This gate is divided into three chapters and explains how to recognize the time of fulfillment.

The first chapter explains why some dreams are fulfilled quickly, and others take longer; the second explains what elements[225] of a dream hint at the time of fulfillment, whether sooner or later; the third explains that it is impossible for the fulfillment of any dream to be delayed more than twenty-two years.

Chapter One

In line with the principles explained above, a righteous person is given advance notice of coming events in order to allow him time to prepare to work toward the dream's fulfillment, and for this reason the fulfillment is often delayed. However, it would be wrong to inform a wicked person of coming events in time to allow him to plan an appropriate course of action, and so he is informed close to the time of fulfillment. This rule applies to everyone, each according to his [spiritual] level.

This point is also made in the Zohar:

If a person is meritorious, his soul ascends Above and sees whatever it sees, but if not, it is seized on that side and is informed of false matters or matters which will soon come to pass.[226]

Scripture, too, verifies this rule, for we see that the dreams of the wicked come to pass quickly, while the fulfillment of the dreams of the righteous is delayed. [R. Almoli cites several cases where this was true, among them the dream of the Midianite soldier in Judges 7:13, when Gideon was about to do battle with Midian.] One of the Midianites dreamed that a loaf of barley bread from the Israelite camp whirled through the Midianite camp; it struck a tent, causing it to fall down. This was interpreted as follows: "That can only mean the sword of the Israelite Gideon son of Joash. God is delivering Midian and the entire camp into his hands."[227] And so it was; the loaf of barley bread represented people [i.e., the Israelites] who are sustained by bread, and with the strength it provided they fell upon the Midianites, attacking and defeating them. [R. Almoli notes that this dream was fulfilled immediately—before the Midianites could beat back the Israelite attack.]

Similarly, the dreams of Pharaoh's Butler and Baker were fulfilled within three days, Pharaoh's dreams were delayed no more than six months, and Nebuchadnezzar's dream a year, as Scripture states, "at the end of twelve months."[228] Jacob's dream, which was prophetic, was never entirely fulfilled, for whatever was going to happen to his sons in the future was already hinted at in it, as one who understands these matters knows, and so too Joseph's dream was not fulfilled until twenty-years had passed.

The nature of the communication further confirms this principle, for it is of greater import to be informed of things that will not come to pass for a century than to know what will transpire in seven years. For this reason, someone who achieves greater [spiritual] perfection will be informed of matters of greater moment than someone of lesser attainments.

Gersonides agreed with this principle in his *Wars of the Lord,* in which he proved that communications regarding imminent matters are less perfect than those pertaining to matters which are not imminent . . . in the manner of daydreams. Likewise, communications regarding imminent things reach the dreamer more readily than others, as we have seen in the many cases of people who panic when they are about to experience an evil which is about to come upon them even though they are not consciously aware of what is in store for them, just as near-sighted people panic when they see the light of a flame, even though they do not see the flame itself.

Chapter Two

Explaining which elements of a dream hint at the time of fulfillment, whether sooner or later.

I once saw the opinion of a certain scholar that things seen in dreams during the first four days of the week will quickly come to pass, either on the day of the dream or within three days, but if they are seen on Thursday or Friday they will not come to pass so quickly; if they appear on the Sabbath, they will be delayed. Others say that one must consider the nature of the stellar configuration and the motion of the moon on the night of the dream; if the moon hurries in its path while in a "moving" constellation of the zodiac,[229] this signifies that the event [forecast by the dream] will occur on that very day, while if the moon tarries on its path within a "stationary" constellation, in particular the constellation of the Bucket,[230] the dream's fulfillment will take a long time. The time of fulfillment corresponds to the number of degrees through which the moon must move before leaving that particular constellation, or the number of degrees through which the moon has already moved through that constellation, in days or months or years. Here there is a wonderful correspondence between matters which occur in this world and the heavenly motions. In most cases, you will find in regard to important matters that the moon is then passing through "stationary" constellations,[231] and tarries, and in regard to unimportant matters that it is hurrying through inverted constellations; in matters of middling importance, it is located within constellations made up of two bodies[232]—unquote.[233]

However, since few people understand the paths of the planets well, and one should not rely on this alone, it is fitting to provide other measures of a dream's fulfillment, and these are four.

First, if the dreamer sees his dream clearly as if he were awake, so that when he awakens he remembers everything he saw in the dream, forgetting none of it, we know that the dream will soon be fulfilled. But if he sees the dream unclearly, and when awake remembers nothing of it, as if he had not dreamed at all,[234] the dream will not be fulfilled so quickly, but only after a long time. If his vision was intermediate, so that he remembers some of the dream and forgets some of it, then the dream will not be fulfilled quickly but not with great delay either. The same holds in regard to the degrees of memory in between these marks; everything depends on how clear the vision is.

Reason dictates that this should be so, for something far away from a person will not be seen as clearly as something close by. Some semblance of a Scriptural proof for this rule may be obtained from Nebuchadnezzar's first dream,[235] for since he had not seen the dream with absolute clarity, he forgot it upon awakening,[236] and so it was not fulfilled until a certain number of years.[237] On the other hand, Nebuchadnezzar's second dream[238] and Pharaoh's dream were clearly seen by the dreamers so that they could be related to the interpreters, and thus they were fulfilled quickly, as Scripture states—"at the end of twelve months"[239] in regard to Nebuchadnezzar's, while as far as Pharaoh's dream is concerned, the years of plenty began immediately after Joseph's appointment as vizier; and so too was the case in regard to the Butler and the Baker.[240]

The second aspect is this. If someone has the same dream two or three times, we know that it will quickly be fulfilled, but if he dreams it but once, then it will not be fulfilled as quickly.

In this instance too there is a semblance of proof from Scripture. Joseph said to Pharaoh: "And regarding the repetition of the dream, for the matter has been determined by God, and God will soon carry it out."[241] But Joseph's and Nebuchadnezzar's dreams, inasmuch as they had them but once,[242] were not fulfilled until some time had passed.

The scholar Amunados[243] discusses a third aspect of this question: how many hours before daybreak the dream occurred. The closer to morning that a dream comes, he maintains, the sooner it will be fulfilled. [This is so certain that Amunados] identified each hour with a month; if the dreamer has his dream three hours before daybreak, it will be fulfilled within three months; so too for other times, whether more or less.

I found support for this view in Genesis Rabba:

R. Yohanan said: "Any dream which occurs close to the morning will come to pass immediately." And so here in regard to Pharaoh's dreams which were close to morning, they were fulfilled immediately; but later on, when [Nebuchadnezzar's dream came] in the evening, [the fulfillment] was delayed a long time.[244]

The origin of this tradition requires investigation. How did the Sages know that Pharaoh's dream occurred close to daybreak, and Nebuchadnezzar's at the beginning of the night?

Presumably they were impelled to this conclusion by Scripture's statement after describing Pharaoh's first dream, "He slept and dreamed a second time," immediately after which it is written, "And it came to pass in the morning."[245]

[This implies that the dreams occurred close to morning.] Regarding Nebuchadnezzar the text does not say this but instead: "His spirit was agitated, and he could not sleep."[246] Apparently he remained awake all night, mulling it over and dozing fitfully, whereas in regard to Joseph's dreams this is not recorded. Thus it seems that Nebuchadnezzar's dream came at the beginning of the night, which then stretched before him.

There is another point, and this is the essential one. It is proper to view the nature of whatever appears in the dream and relate it to the dreamer's life, in order to determine whether its prompt fulfillment is at all possible given the dreamer's situation. This aspect of dream interpretation arises from the conjecture we made above (in the last gate) regarding the relevance of the circumstances of the dreamer's life. There we explained that this is how Joseph understood that the dreams of the Chief Baker and Butler would soon be fulfilled, for he knew that but three days remained until Pharaoh's birthday [when it was likely that decisions regarding their fates would be made]. As for Joseph's dreams concerning his future greatness, an interpreter would quite properly recognize that in the nature of the matter they could not be fulfilled within a short period, at least not until the relevant circumstances had come to pass and the proper people were in place.

Chapter Three, in which it is explained that no dream's fulfillment may be delayed more than twenty-two years. We learned in Chapter "He Who Sees" [i.e., Berakhot, chapter 9, the so-called "Tractate on Dreams"]:

Said R. Levi: A person should always look to [the fulfillment] of a favorable dream [as long as] twenty-two years. From where do we know [this]? From Joseph, as is written, "These are the generations of Jacob: Joseph was seventeen years old," etc.[247] and it is further written, "And Joseph was thirty years old when he stood before Pharaoh."[248] How many years is it from seventeen to thirty? Thirteen. Add the seven years of plenty and the two years of famine [at which point Joseph met his brothers again], and you have twenty-two [years from the time he dreamed his dreams to the time they were fulfilled, when his brothers bowed before him].[249]

The point of this statement is clear. It comes to inform us of two important principles in dream interpretation. The first is what Gersonides wrote in his *Wars of the Lord*:[250] dreams only concern things that will happen soon and not things that are far off in the future. Experience confirms this; we most often dream about what will happen to us on the very day of the dream or the day after, for we are not on a [spiritual] level that merits more advanced warning.

The second principle to be learned from this Talmudic statement is that even when a dream's fulfillment is delayed, it is not delayed more than twenty-two years.

We must, however, ask how the Sages know that when a dream is delayed it may not be delayed more than twenty-two years. While the fulfillment of Joseph's dream was not delayed for more than twenty-two years, who can say that there is no dream whose fulfillment is delayed longer? Perhaps Joseph's dream was of the sort whose fulfillment is fairly quick, or perhaps it was one of those which is delayed a middling amount of time, and there are dreams delayed still longer. Moreover, we have found many dreams which were not fulfilled for many long years, as in the case of the dream of the Chief Butler, according to the interpretations which the Sages themselves put forth, may their memory be blessed, and the dream of Nebuchadnezzar, which has yet to be entirely fulfilled! This requires more thought.

Furthermore, consider the phrase "favorable dream" in this statement. Does it mean that a favorable dream will not be delayed more than twenty-two years, but an unfavorable one will? Or perhaps this distinction was not intended? If we hold that the distinction was intended, and an unfavorable dream's fulfillment may be delayed longer, could we not say that the reason for this is that the Holy One, blessed be He, holds back His anger, hoping that the dreamer will repent and the decree announced by the dream be annulled? After all, God's grace is greater than His intent to punish, and the latter will not annul His good intention.[251] As our Sages said, the good intent is not taken back, even when it is only announced as a possibility,[252] and certainly if it is positively decreed.

This gate is complete, as are the other gates of this part, God be thanked.

The Second Part

In this part I record all the solutions of dreams—what each one teaches. In order to give over each one according to its author, I begin by listing the sources from which I have drawn what follows. First, I draw on the words of our Sages in the Talmud, may their memory be blessed;[253] second, the word of R. Hai Gaon, may his memory be blessed, in his "Gates for the Explanation of Dreams"; third, the explanation of dreams I found attributed to Rashi; fourth, a book attributed to the righteous Joseph;[254] fifth, explanations attributed to Daniel—it is said that he composed them in Babylonia in the days of Nebuchadnezzar; since people begged him to inform them of these matters, he acceded to their request. Furthermore, I found dream interpretations translated from the books of the gentiles. Again, I found anonymous books of dream interpretations. It seems to me that both these categories of books are alike the words of the wise, but some were attributed to famous historical figures who were known as great dream interpreters.[255] In any case, I have copied them all and arranged them in order, giving their origins at the end, except for those which are anonymous. . . . In some cases I also explain the relationship between the interpretation and the dream itself, especially when the interpretation seems inverted.

However, it is worthwhile to tell you what I have concluded in this respect, namely, that all of these interpretations are built on one or another of the great Kabbalistic principles. After all, the Rabbis of the Talmud were great Kabbalistic Sages, as was R. Hai Gaon, and it was out of his great Kabbalistic knowledge that he wrote these explanations.

The other Sages and prophets, too, were all Kabbalists, and derived their interpretations from the wisdom of Kabbalah. I have found support for this in the Zohar, which gives a Kabbalistic explanation of some of the interpretations mentioned in the Talmud.

They said in Parashat Terumah:

> We have learned: Whoever sees grapes in his dream, if they are white, it is well; if they are black, and ripe, it is well; if unripe, mercy is required. What is the difference between white and black, ripe and unripe? We further

learnt: [If] he ate the black ones, it is certain that he has a portion in the world
to come. However, we also learnt: The tree which was the occasion of
Adam's sin was a grapevine, as is written, "His grapes are bitter grapes."[256]
These black grapes and white grapes which are good, for they come from
the side of Life, but those black grapes, [regarding which it is said] that mercy
is required, for they are from the side of Death. Ripe—it is well, since at a
time that white ones predominate without fragrance, for at that time all
require *tikkun*; though all are good, without *tikkun,* black and white are
intermixed, and at times when the white ones do not predominate, and black
ones are seen, it should be known that they have appeared [symbolizing] a
judgment of death, and mercy is required, for the tree in regard to which
Adam sinned caused death to him and to the entire world.

There are many similar interpretations in that work, and they seem to have
been produced on the basis of Kabbalistic wisdom.

The discussion that follows is divided into five gates, each corresponding
to one category of created entities: inanimate substances, plants, animals, man,
supernal creations. Each gate is further subdivided into chapters appropriate to
its subject.

Gate One, containing five chapters,
arranged according to the order of inanimate objects

I. The element of earth, e.g., lands and borders, states and places.
II. The element of water, e.g., seas, pools, ritual baths, rain and snow.
III. The element of air.
IV. The element of fire.
V. Inanimate objects made of mixtures of elements, e.g., minerals.

Gate Two, regarding plants,
containing five chapters

I. Seeds.
II. Trees.
III. Fruits.
IV. Products which issue from them, such as wine and oil.
V. Ships.

Gate Three, regarding animals,
containing six chapters

I. Domestic animals
II. Wild animals.

III. Birds.
IV. Fish.
V. Animal products, e.g., milk, cheese, eggs, bee honey.
VI. Cooked dishes made from these.

Gate Four, regarding mankind,
containing five chapters

I. Ordinary people.
II. Kings and nobles.
III. Women.
IV. The dead.
V. Clothers
.

Gate Five, regarding supernal creations,
containing three chapters

I. Sun, moon, and stars.
II. Thunder.
III. Books, for the Divine Torah is from heaven.

Note: The order of entries in this part follows the Jerusalem, 1965 edition of *Pitron Halomot.*

Gate One
Inanimate Objects[257]

Chapter One
Earth

If you see yourself digging in the earth with a healthy body, there is no need for concern.

If you see yourself digging in the earth while ill, it is a bad sign.

The explanation: Even though you may appear to be digging your grave, you are healthy, so there is no need for concern; if you are ill, however, it is a bad sign.

If you see yourself carrying earth, it is a bad sign. Explanation: a hint of burial.

Geographical Locations[258]

If you see yourself in the land of:

Edom—troubles will come upon you.

Aram—you have sinned.

The Land of Israel—God will lead you there.

Germany—a bereavement will occur.

Damascus and its rivers—God will renew your life.

Ham—troubles will come upon you but you will survive.

Jerusalem—God will give you a post of authority.

Jordan—your lot is with the righteous.

Ethiopia—you will find yourself in great trouble.

A metropolis—you see yourself entering a metropolis in peace; your needs are being met, as is written, "He leads him to his destination."[259]

A fortress—you will perform a deed for which God will protect you.

The East—you will receive benefits.

The West[260]—you will travel to a faraway land and return.

Egypt—you will receive great good.

Philistia—you will perform a deed for which God will draw you near to Himself. Explanation: Just as Avimelekh, king of the Philistines, drew near to Abraham and made a treaty with him.

Seir—illness will come upon you.

If you see yourself in a country whose name begins with:

A—you will be well.

B—you will build a house.[261]

G—God will bestow good on you.

D—a banner of kindness will flutter over you.

H—God will prepare the way for you.

V—woe to you!

Z—God has prepared happiness and wealth for you.

Ch—illness will come upon you.

Tet—if you move to another country, you will become wealthy.

Y—God will protect you.

K—a way is being prepared for you from Above.

L—there is hope.

M—your sustenance is assured and your enemies will fall before you.

N—your domicile will be at peace.

S—God will support you because He loves you.

Ayin—God is watching over you.

P—God will redeem you from trouble.

Tzaddik—you are a righteous man.

Q—God is near.

R—you will see that which your heart desires.

Sh—God will answer your prayer.

T—you are forthright.[262]

A city:

If you see yourself in an unwalled city, troubles will pass you by.

If you see yourself moving from one city to another, you will travel long distances.

If you see yourself returning home, your well-being will increase.

House:

If you see yourself at home or in your city, you will be saved from trouble.

If you see yourself destroying a new house, it is a bad sign.

If you see yourself destroying an old house, it is a good sign.

That is to say: an old house is a bad sign in a dream, and when you see it destroyed, that is good, for the evil is driven away. Conversely, a new house is a good sign, and when you see it destroyed, happiness is driven away, and it is a bad sign.

A well-decorated house, this foretells happiness and tranquility.

A wall:

If you see a wall in your house fall, death and trouble are near; that is to say, since a man's principal residence is in his house, when the wall of the house falls, it is a sign that the house will be destroyed without any inhabitant remaining. Since its inhabitants will die, others will flee from it.

Roof:

If you see yourself going up to the roof, you will rise to eminence.

If you see yourself descending from the roof, you will lose your eminence.

Abaye and Rava both say: Once he ascends to eminence, he retains his position.[263]

Door:

If you set up a door in the doorway of your house, you will soon marry a woman.

If you see the threshold of your house broken, either your children or your wife will die.

Trees or wooden supports:

If you see the trees which support your house broken, it is a bad sign.

Beams:

If you see the beams of your house fall, a child will die.

Ceiling:

If you see the ceiling fall, your wife will die.

Mountain:

We learn in the Talmud: Whoever sees a mountain should rise early and say: "How pleasant on the mountains, etc."[264] before some other verse occurs to him, such as "I will mourn on the mountains,"[265] God forbid.

If you see yourself ascending a mountain, you will rise to eminence.

If you see yourself descending a mountain, it is a bad sign.

If you see yourself standing on a mountain, you will see greatness for yourself.

If you see the mountain quake, evil will come upon you at that moment.

A high place:

If you see yourself in a high place, you will attain the friendship of high officials.

If you see yourself looking out from a high place, it signifies a long life.

If you see yourself ascending to a high place, it is a good sign for you and your children.

A narrow place:

If you see yourself suddenly standing in a narrow place, you will profit, a good sign. [Comment:] I do not know why; on the contrary, I have heard from many, and I too have had some experience of this, that seeing oneself enclosed in a place from where there is no exit or struggling out of a narrow hole, above or below, all indicate trouble for the dreamer.

A ladder:

If you see yourself ascending a ladder, it is a good sign.

Arrested by an officer:

Arrested by an officer, you are being guarded from harm.[266]

If you are put in chains, your protection is being increased. This refers specifically to being put in chains, but not a rope. Explanation: one who is handed over to an officer is thereby kept from fleeing, and if you see this in a dream, it is a sign that you are being guarded from harm.

Chapter Two
The Element of Water

Marsh:

Whoever enters a marsh in a dream will become head of the Yeshiva. R. Papa and R. Huna son of R. Yehoshua had dreams. R. Papa dreamed that he had entered a marsh and subsequently became head of the yeshiva. R. Huna dreamed that he had entered a wood and subsequently became the head of the kallah.[267] Others say: Both dreamed about entering a marsh, but R. Papa, who was carrying a drum,[268] became head of the yeshiva, while R. Huna, who was not carrying a drum, became head of the kallah. R. Ashi said: I dreamed that I went into a marsh carrying a drum and beat the drum.[269]

The explanation of all this is that a marsh contains reeds crowded together; this symbolizes the head of the yeshiva, whose students gather together and come to hear his lectures,[270] while the woods have large trees next to one another, which represent the head of the teacher's students, who, as the students review the lecture, explains to them whatever they do not understand.

As for the dreams, it is not necessarily the case that both entered a marsh. The essential difference is that R. Ashi had a bell and clapper hanging from his neck, the symbol of a head of the yeshiva, whose arrival is announced, while R. Huna did not, but merely entered the marsh and so became the head of the kallah. . . .

Well:

Whoever sees a well in a dream, R. Hanina said: He will see peace, as it is written, "Isaac's servants dug in the valley and found a well of living waters there."[271] R. Nathan said: He will find Torah, as it is written, "Whoever finds me finds life,"[272] and it is written, "a well of living water."[273] Rava said: It literally means life.[274]

If you see a well in a dream, rise early and recite the following verse: "Isaac's servants dug in the valley and found a well of living waters there"[275] before another verse occurs to you, "For distress will come in like a river."[276]

Rain:

If you see rain in a dream, it is a sign of improved circumstances; others say: a sign of dispute.

If you drink rainwater, it signifies joy.

If you are standing in the rain, it signifies good tidings.

And Rashi writes: Whoever sees rain descending heavily at an unusual time, this means that a decree will come on that country. If it comes in its proper season, greatness will be announced for that country.

Mud:

If you see yourself swimming in mud in a dream and drowning, troubles will come upon you but you will be saved from them.

If you see yourself passing over mud, there will be a dispute.

If you see yourself muddied, it signifies illness or loss of money. Others say: troubles will come upon you but you will be saved from them.

If you see yourself falling into mud, illness will befall you but you will be healed.

The sea:

If you see the sea rushing to drown you, you will fall into the power of your enemies and they will treat you harshly (Rashi).

If you see the sea receding and drying up, the ruler of that country will be removed.

If you see the sea receding, an official of that country will die (Rashi).

If you see yourself walking on foot in the sea, do not travel on foot on that day.

If you see yourself bathing in the sea, it signifies tranquility.

And if the water is turgid, you will argue with your superior.

If you see yourself swimming in the sea or a pool or in a river or in a ritual bath, you will join together with good men.

And Rashi writes: If you see yourself swimming in a river or in the sea, and the sea raises large waves, you will receive benefit from a great king.

If you see yourself swimming in a brook, you will join with a righteous man; if he drinks from it, great benefit will come to you.

If you see yourself drowning in the sea, it signifies illness or loss of money. Others say: Trouble will come upon him but he will be saved. And still others say: He should beg for mercy, for otherwise he might die.

And Rashi writes: If you see yourself running into the sea and drowning, you will fall into the power of an evil king who will trouble you.

If you see yourself falling into the sea, illness will befall you but you will be healed.

If you see yourself falling into the sea or a river and cannot rise, there will be bereavement.

Woods:

If you see yourself entering a wood, you will become the head of the kallah.[277]

Water:

If you see yourself drinking water, it is a good sign.

If you see yourself drinking cold water, so may it happen to you; others say: His money will increase.

If you drink spring water in a dream, very great benefit will come to you.

If you drink wormwood, it signifies a dispute.

A bathhouse:

If you see a bathhouse, you will be saved from trouble. Others say: it is a good sign.

If you enter a bathhouse, you will be saved from evil people.

If you see yourself as the owner of a bathhouse and a book, you will attain greatness, for people will wonder at you.

If you see yourself bathing in a bathhouse, trouble will pass over you (R. Hai Gaon).

If you see yourself leaving a bathhouse, you will be saved from trouble.

A stream or spring:

If you bathe in a spring, it is a good sign.

If you see a stream flowing softly, there will be peace.

If it is rushing, fear your enemies and keep away from them.

In the Talmud: One who sees a river in his dreams should rise early and say, "Behold, I will extend peace to her like a river,"[278] before another verse occurs to him, "For distress will come in like a river."[279]

If you are bathing in a river, it is a bad sign.

If you see yourself fall into a river and cannot rise, it signifies bereavement.

If you see yourself being swept away by a stream, take care not to do any wrong, lest you be given over to the powers that be.

Washing:

If you see yourself bathing in hot water, trouble will pass you by.

If you see yourself bathing in lukewarm water, it signifies joy.

If you see yourself bathing in cold water, your troubles will diminish and you will receive good tidings.

If you see yourself bathing in a spring, it is a good sign.

If you see yourself in a bathhouse, it signifies tranquility. But if the water is roiled, you will argue with your superior.

Chapter Three
Regarding the Element of Air

If you see yourself swept up by the wind, you will have rulership. Others say: desolation.

Chapter Four
The Element of Fire

Fire, which is destructive and untamed, points to trouble sent by God to a nation or to the ruler, but if the fire is domesticated for human use, as in candles, etc., it denotes various things, depending on the context (R. Hai Gaon).

Fire:

If you see fire descending, there will be plague in your country.

Explanation: Just as fire consumes, so does plague kill.

If you see yourself falling into a fire, you will abandon God's will.

Explanation: You are destined for the fires of Gehenna.

A house set afire:

If you see your house set afire, you will be involved in a dispute.

Coals:

If you walk on glowing coals, your body will be impaired.

If you see dying embers, this denotes a dispute with enemies.

Lamp:

If you see a lamp alight in your room, you will marry a new wife.

Explanation: Because a wife is the light of the house.

If you see a darkened lamp, your wife will die, may God protect you both.

Chapter Five
Minerals

Crystal:

If you see pure crystal, God loves you.

Gold:

If you find gold, you will attain eminence.

If you see yourself finding a golden vessel, you will be honored.

If you see that a golden vessel has been taken from you, whatever evil has been said about you and all that your enemies wish on you will come to pass.

If you see yourself worshiping a golden idol, you will come to a situation in which you will be hated. And some say: All dreams of gold represent trouble for you, and you will have trouble with people.

A seal:

If you see a seal without pearls, you will accomplish a praiseworthy act.

A ring:

If you see a ring without pearls, you will accomplish a praiseworthy act.

If you see a silver seal-ring, you will attain so much eminence that strangers will envy you.

If you see a ring on one of your fingers, except for the pinkie, you will be an object of suspicion.

If you see yourself given a ring as a gift, it is a good sign (R. Hai Gaon).

If you see a silver or crystal ring, it is a good sign. If it is iron, even better, for you will suddenly gain a great profit (Daniel).

If you see fifty rings on your fingers, you will attain rulership.

Glass vessels:

If you see that glass vessels have fallen before you and broken, whatever evil has been said about you and all that your enemies wish upon you will come to pass.

Silver:

All types of silver, a good sign.

If you see yourself worshiping a silver idol, you will come to a situation in which you will be hated.

If you see yourself finding silver or gold, you will be honored.

If you find silver, it is a good sign.

A crown:

If you see a silver or gold crown, and you are an artisan, it is a good sign; if not, it is a bad sign.

A coin:

If you see a whole coin, you will be wealthy.

If you see many gold coins, it signifies evil. And some say: whoever sees silver and gold coins, an improvement in his circumstances.

If you see yourself finding a copper coin, you will be involved in a dispute.

If you see yourself finding hidden coins, you will gain great benefit.

If you lost them or found them broken, trouble will befall you.

Finds:

If you find something in a dream, and you are wealthy, you will become poor.

If you see yourself finding silver and gold vessels, you will be honored.

If you see yourself finding iron articles, such as nails and spits, you will have a great dispute with your family.

If you find silver or silver vessels, it is a good sign.

If you find a copper penny, you will be involved in a dispute.

A pearl:

If you see pearls, honor and authority will be yours. Others say: tears.

Metal:

The Talmud says: All types of metal implements are good in a dream, except for hoes, mattocks, and hatchets. This applies only if they have their handles attached. [Explanation:] Because they are fit for their work, to destroy and harm.

All types of iron implements, a good sign, except for shovels and scalpels. Others add: nails and pans.

An idol:

If you see yourself worshiping a silver or gold idol, you will come to a situation in which you are hated.

And if the idol is bronze or iron, evil can be expected of you.[280]

If it is made of wood, you will become poor.

Gate Two
Vegetation

Chapter One
Seeds

If you see yourself eating:

Melons—sickness will befall you.

Peas, beans—your circumstances will improve.

Onions or leeks, cooked or raw, you will have pains.
Explanation: Because they are unhealthy (*Sefer Yosef ha-Tzaddik*).

Vegetables taken from a garden plot which you are shown—you will incur a bad reputation. Others say: His wife is committing adultery (*Daniel*).

Gourds:

The Talmud reports: Only one who is pious is shown gourds.[281] Explanation: Because the Hebrew word *dala'at*, "gourd," is related to *dalu,* as in the expression "My eyes are raised to heaven."[282]

Horseradish—you will have a good life (Rashi).

Wheat—your circumstances will improve, it foretells of an increase of silver and gold. Explanation: It is written, "the fat of wheat will satisfy you."[283] And in the Talmud: Rabbah bar Bar Hana said in the name of R. Yohanan: Whoever sees wheat in a dream will see peace, as it is written: "Who makes your boundary peaceful, the fat of wheat will satisfy you."[284] And from R. Hai Gaon: Whoever sees a stalk of green wheat will see his circumstances improve.

Vegetables with bread—you will incur a bad reputation; others say: he will be well.

Herbs and vinegar—a bad sign.

If you see yourself selling herbs, your business will diminish (R. Hai Gaon). All types of vegetables are good signs in a dream, except turnip-tops, onions, and garlic. And in the Talmud: In general all types of vegetables are good signs in a dream, except for turnip-tops. But did not R. Ashi say: "I saw a turnip in a dream and became rich"? There he saw it still in the ground, while R. Ashi saw it in the stalk.[285]

Cabbage:

If you see cabbage and other cooked vegetables, it is a good sign and wealth will come to you (R. Hai Gaon).

Bread:

If you see yourself eating a clean loaf [made of well-strained flour, without foreign admixtures], be assured that you have a portion in the world to come (*Sefer Yosef ha-Tzaddik*).

Bread and vegetables—you will incur a bad reputation.[286]

Fine wheat bread—be assured that your prayer will be answered.

Turnips—things will be difficult.

Bitter herbs—a bad sign.

Grass—you will find your sustenance, and will be well.[287]

Radish—your circumstances will improve, and a good life will be yours (Rashi).

Flour:

If you see yourself holding flour in your hand, your circumstances will improve (*Daniel*).

Cucumbers—illness will befall you.[288]

Stalks of grain:

If you see yourself reaping stalks, your circumstances will improve.

A field:

If you see yourself in a field which has been sown, this foretells good times. Explanation: Because of the stalks which touch you.

Garlic:

If you see garlic, it signifies problems.[289]

Barley:

If you see barley, your sins will depart, as it is written: "Your sin is taken away, and your iniquity is atoned."[290] R. Zera said: "I did not go up [from Babylon] to the land of Israel until I saw barley in a dream."[291]

Chapter Two
Trees and Their Fruits

Nuts signify a hard person, and his shadow—that is, his company—is evil.
Trees:[292]
If you see a fruit tree uprooted, trouble will befall you.
If you see a tree moved from its place, you will go to another place.
If you see trees in a dream, it is a bad sign for you and your house. Explanation: "Is the man a tree of the field to come before you in a siege?"[293]
If you see yourself surrounded by trees, you will have children.
If you climb a tree, honor will come your way.
If you see trees falling, your children will die.
If you see a tree fall, you will have problems and will fear someone, either a great person or the ruler of the city or a king, but you will not be able to go somewhere else in order to save yourself.
If you see trees blooming, it is a good sign.
If you see fruit on trees, attach yourself to a great person and derive benefit from him.[294]
If you see yourself sleeping under a tree, God will help you. Others say: You will have children.
If you see trees being uprooted, it portends war and panic.
Cedars:[295]
If you see cedars broken, it is a very bad sign; fast in order to save yourself from evil decrees.
A vine:
If you see a vine bearing grapes, your wife will not miscarry, as it is written, "Your wife is a fruitful vine."[296]
[If you see a choice vine,] look forward to the Messiah, as it is written, "Hitching his foal to a vine and his she-donkey to a choice vine."[297]
In general, vines and date palms symbolize one's wives, since they are very fruitful; the date palm in particular denotes a woman of importance.
Myrtle:
"If you see a myrtle, your property will prosper," as the Talmud states. Explanation: Like the myrtle, whose leaves are intertwined. "'If he has no

79

property, he will receive an inheritance from elsewhere,' [so says] Ulla. Others say, R. Joshua ben Levi[298]—this is only if you see the myrtle on its stem."[299]

Vineyard:

If you see yourself planting a vineyard, it is a good sign.

If you see a vineyard without grapes and stroll in it, it signifies mourning.

Lulav:

If you see a lulav, you are wholehearted for your Father in Heaven.[300]

A plant:

If you see yourself leaning over a plant, it is a good sign.

If you see a plant in flower, it is a good sign for you and for your wife.

Logs:

If you see long logs, it signifies satiety and contentment.

Beams:

If you see a broken beam, it is a bad sign. Fast, repent completely, and you will be saved.

If you see a pillar fall, you will have trouble and fear someone, either a great person or the ruler of the city or a king, but you will not be able to go someplace else in order to save yourself.

Reed:

[The Talmud says:] Whoever sees a reed should look forward to wisdom, as it is written, "Acquire wisdom."[301] If he sees several reeds, he may look forward to understanding, since it is written, "With all your gettings, get understanding."[302]

If you see a reed, rise early and say, "A bruised reed shall not break,"[303] before another verse occurs to you, "Behold, you trust the staff of this bruised reed."[304]

R. Zera said: A gourd, a palm-heart, wax, and a reed are all good signs in a dream.

Fig tree:

If you see a fig tree, your Torah knowledge will be preserved within you, as it is written, "He who keeps the fruit tree will eat the fruit thereof."[305]

Palm:

See Vine.

Apple tree:

If you see an apple tree which has sweet apples, this denotes a person both good and wealthy. If they are sour, this denotes a wicked, sour person.

Chapter Three
Fruit

Nuts:

If you see yourself eating nuts, you will have a good life.

If you see yourself receiving nuts, it is a sign of honor with jealousy.

Pears:

If you see yourself eating pears or quinces, you will live a good life.

Citron (etrog):

If you see a citron, you will be honored by your Creator, as it is said, "the fruit of a glorious tree."[306]

Peanuts:

If you see yourself eating dried or fresh peanuts, your troubles will renew themselves.

Cherries:

If you see yourself eating cherries, you will fall ill and recover.

Explanation: Because they are one of the things which enter the body but from which the body receives no benefit.[307]

Olives:

[The Talmud says]: Whoever sees olives in a dream, if they are little ones, his business will be fruitful and increase like an olive. This is if he sees the fruit, but if he sees the trees, he will have many sons, as it is written, "Your children like olive plants, round your table."[308] Others say: Whoever sees an olive in his dream will acquire a good name, as it is written, "The Lord called your name a leafy olive tree, fair and good fruit."[309] [Whoever sees olive oil in a dream may hope for the light of the Torah, as it is written, "That they bring to you pure olive oil beaten for the light"[310]].[311]

Ginger:

If you see yourself eating ginger, God is satisfied with you (R. Hai Gaon). In other books: If you see ginger or a fowl, your name is known all over the world. Explanation: For all need you, and like you, and whoever is beloved [by people] is beloved by God,[312] and your reputation goes before you when you are brought from place to place.

Lemon:

If you see yourself eating lemon, you will become poor.

Crab apples:

If you eat red crab apples in a dream, illness will befall you.

If you eat white crab apples in a dream, you will come into property and wealth.

Grapes:

[The Talmud says:] Whoever sees grapes [in a dream] should rise early and recite, "[I found Israel] like grapes in the wilderness,"[313] before another verse occurs to him—"their grapes were grapes of gall."[314]

[The Talmud says:] Whoever sees grapes in a dream, if they are white, whether in season or not in season, they are a good sign; if black, and in season, they are a good sign, if not in season, they are a bad sign, [and heavenly mercy is required. If he sees himself eating these, he can be certain that he has a portion in the world to come.][315] Explanation: this hints at the "wine which is stored in its grapes from the Seven Days of Creation" [to be consumed by the righteous in the Messianic age]. If they are red, it is a good sign for him and his children.

Others say: If you eat grapes in a dream, do not appear before a judge or an official, for if you do, your enemies will prevail.

Fruit:

[The Talmud says:] All types of fruit are good [signs] in a dream, except for dates.[316] Explanation: Because they have not altogether ripened.

If you see early fruits, greatness will be yours.

Pepper:

If you see yourself eating peppers, you will have status before the king.

Raisins:

If you see raisins, your situation will improve. Explanation: When grapes are fresh they rot and sometimes one has a loss from them. But when they are raisins, they last and one has no loss, but will profit.

Pomegranates:

[The Talmud states:] Whoever sees pomegranates in a dream, and they are little ones, his business will be as fruitful as a pomegranate; if they are big, his business will increase like a pomegranate. If they are split open, and he is a scholar, he may look forward to learning more Torah, as it is written: "I would make you drink spiced wine, of the juice of my pomegranates";[317] if he is unlearned, he may look forward to performing mitzvot, as it is written, "Your temples are like a pomegranate split open."[318] What is meant by "your temples"? Even those of you who are devoid [of learning] are full of mitzvot like a pomegranate.[319]

Almonds:
If you see yourself eating fresh, sour almonds, illnesses will bypass you.

Figs:
If you see black figs, it is a sign of oppression.

If you see yourself eating fresh figs, you will earn money in business (R. Hai Gaon).

If you see yourself eating dried figs, it signifies an improvement in your circumstances.

Dates:
If you see dates, it is a good sign, but do not appear before an official or a ruler (*Daniel*).

[The Talmud says:] Whoever sees dates, his sins will be at an end, as it is written, "Your sins are at an end, [O daughter of Zion]."[320]

If you see yourself eating dates, troubles will bypass you. Explanation: suffering mitigates sin.

Apples:
If you see yourself eating apples, a good life will be yours, great status will come to you.

In other books: If you eat an apple, it is a sign of trouble. Elsewhere: a sign of illness.

Chapter Four
Products Which Issue from Them

Wine:
If you drink spiced wine in a dream, it is a sign of financial loss.
Wine-press:
If you see a wine-press, it signifies tidings of rain, but there will be a dispute over the wine-press.

If you see yourself pressing grapes, security and property will be yours (Rashi). Others say: Wealth will be yours.[321]

If you see a wine-press pressing wine, it is a sign of dispute.

If you see a barrel of wine, great joy will soon befall you.
Date wine:
If you drink date wine, you will have property and wealth (R. Hai Gaon).
Wine banquet:
If you see yourself invited to a banquet at which wine is drunk, illnesses will befall you; but if you do not drink with them, you will be saved from your illness.

If you see yourself at a banquet, a [financial] loss will befall you.

If you see yourself drinking wine-lees, great pain will befall you.
Beverages:
[The Talmud says: A Tanna recited in the presence of R. Yohanan:] All types of beverages are good signs in a dream, except for wine; sometimes one may drink it and it turns out well, and sometimes one may drink and it turns out badly. Sometimes one may drink it and it turns out well, as it is written, "Wine gladdens the heart of man."[322] Sometimes one may drink it and it turns out badly, as it is written, "Give strong drink to one about to perish, and wine to the bitter in soul."[323] Said R. Yohanan [to the Tanna]: Teach that for a scholar it is always good, as it is written, "Come eat of my bread and drink of the wine which I have poured,"[324] and if you want, I can say: "I will make you drink spiced wine."[325]

Drunkenness:

If you see yourself drunk, you will have great trouble but be saved from it.

If you see a drunk, your situation will improve.

Intoxicating beverages:

If you see all types of intoxicating beverages, you will have property and wealth.

If you see yourself drinking intoxicating beverages made from wheat, healing and money will come to you.

If you see yourself drinking intoxicating beverages made from grain, reward and wealth will come to you.

Olive oil:

[The Talmud says:] Whoever sees olive oil may look forward to the light of Torah, as it is written, "and take for yourself olive oil,"[326] and R. Hai Gaon says: Whoever sees himself drinking olive oil, his wife is committing adultery, and he is guilty of fornication; others say: either himself or his wife.

Drinking:

If you see yourself drinking, be careful of anything that falls or that you may fall over.[327]

Chapter Five
Regarding Boats,
Which May Also Be of Wood

If you see ships, this denotes satiety, lordship, and rulership.

If you see a ship with its mast fallen into the Great Sea or see yourself falling while aboard a ship, you will be saved from every trouble.

If you see yourself going aboard a ship, you will go to a distant land; others say: He and his children will be of the world to come. So it is written in *Sefer Yosef ha-Tzaddik,* except that he distinguishes between small boats, in which case the dreamer alone is of the world to come, and large boats, regarding which the dreamer and his children are of the world to come.

If you see yourself sitting on the mast of a ship, and the ship is proceeding under sail,[328] your greatness and wealth will vastly increase.

If you see yourself standing aboard a ship which is docked at its destination, you may hope for great prosperity (R. Hai Gaon).

And from the Talmud: Whoever sits in a small boat will acquire a great reputation; if a large boat, both he and all his family will acquire one. But this is only if it is on the high seas.[329] Explanation: In the depth of the seas, and this is because a ship travels throughout the world, and if it is large, it travels even farther [than a small boat].

If you see yourself sitting aboard a small ship, it is a good sign and you will become the patron[330] of your city.

If you see yourself sitting aboard a boat even though it is not your usual practice, you will go to jail.

If you see yourself falling from a ship into the sea or a river, you will fall into the power of your enemies, who will do you harm; Rashi writes that if he falls into a boat, God will save you from trouble.

If you see a ship which has sunk, you will be saved from all your sins and iniquities; they have descended to the depths of the sea and you will be saved from the judgment of Gehenna (R. Hai Gaon and others).

If you see yourself aboard a large ship, be assured that you have a portion in the world to come.

And if the ship is sinking and you are saved, you will be forgiven all your sins. In other books the following is added: all evil plans against you will be annulled.

If you see yourself falling from a ship into the harbor, it is a good sign (R. Hai Gaon and others).

If you see yourself disembarking from a ship onto dry land, you will be exiled from place to place.

Gate Three
Living Things

Chapter One
Ritually Clean Animals

Sheep:
If you see an ox or a sheep, it is a good sign.

Flocks of sheep:
If you see yourself herding or buying sheep, your sons and daughters will increase (R. Hai Gaon). Elsewhere: If you see yourself herding flocks of sheep, your family and your city will attain eminence.

Rams:
If you see rams, the rain will be plentiful and you will be blessed by it. If you see them gore you, you will rise to greatness and help many people.

Goats:
If you see yourself herding or buying goats, your sons and daughters will increase (R. Hai Gaon).

If you see them goring you or see yourself drinking their milk, your sustenance will be great, as it is written: "And a sufficiency of goat's milk as your food."[331]

And in the Talmud: Said R. Yosef: Whoever sees a goat will have a blessed year. [If he sees several] goats, he will have blessed years, as it is written, "And a sufficiency of goat's milk as your food."[332]

Cows:
If you see oxen or cows, you will see the downfall of your enemies.

Bulls:
If you see cows grazing in the meadow, it is a sign of joy and improved circumstances. If they are sleeping, it signifies laziness and hard times.

An ox:
If you see an ox, you will have a good reputation (R. Hai Gaon); others say: He will attain greatness.

If you see yourself riding on a black ox, greatness will be yours.

If you see an ox plowing, someone who has become distant from you will be friendly again.

If you see yourself riding and fall off your beast, a death will soon affect you. If you see an ox riding on you, you yourself will die that year. If the ox kicks you, you will travel a great distance. If you suck milk from a cow, you will receive a great benefit and enter into a good year. If you bite an ox, you will be lost on the way; if the ox bites you, you will live a long time. If an ox tramples you, you will fall severely ill (R. Hai Gaon).

If you see an ox, whether carrying a load or not, whether pulling a wagon or not, you will hear joyful news (R. Hai Gaon).

Others say: If you ride on an ox while traveling, great troubles will befall you.

If you ride on an ox, you will attain great honor; but if you fall, poverty (*Sefer Yosef ha-Tzaddik*).

In the Talmud: Our Rabbis taught: Five things were said in regard to an ox in a dream. One who eats of its flesh will become rich; if an ox gores him, he will have sons who will debate each other in matters of Torah; if an ox bites him, suffering will befall him; if it kicks him, he will have to go on a long journey; if he rides upon one, he will attain greatness. But has it not been also taught: If he dreams that he rode upon one, he will die? There is no contradiction; in one case he rides on the ox; in the other, the ox rides upon him.[333]

If you see an ox in a dream, rise early and say, "His firstborn ox, majesty is his"[334] before another verse occurs to you, "If an ox gore a man."[335]

Ritually Unclean Animals

Camel:
In the Talmud: If one sees a camel in a dream, Heaven has decreed death for him and he has been saved from it. R. Hama bar Hanina said: What is the verse for this? "I will go down with you to Egypt, and I will also surely bring you up again."[336] (Explanation: *Gam alo'*, "I will surely bring you up again," is an acronym for *gamal*, camel.") R. Nahman bar Isaac derives it from here: "God also put away your sin; you shall not die."[337]

Elsewhere: If you see a camel, it is a sign that the circumstances of your partnership will improve. Still others say: If you see several camels, you will be told bad things.

If you see groups of camels, it is a bad sign.

If you see yourself leading one camel in a group of camels, your luck will change for the better (*Sefer Yosef ha-Tzaddik* and Rashi).

If you see a camel, you will conquer your enemies (Rashi).

If you see yourself riding on a camel, whether male or female, you will travel a great distance (*Sefer Yosef ha-Tzaddik* and Rashi).

If you see yourself falling from a camel, you will become seriously ill (R. Hai Gaon).

If you see a camel kick you, you will hear news (R. Hai Gaon).

If you see yourself kill a camel, you will kill your enemies.

If you eat camel meat or drink camel milk, you will become very rich. Others say: If you eat it, your situation will improve.

Pig:

If you see a pig, good earnings are prepared for you (Daniel).

If you see yourself eating pig's meat, you will add wealth to your wealth (Daniel).

If you see yourself riding a pig, you will be protected from your enemies, and if you eat its meat, it is a good sign.

Donkey:

If you see a donkey expect the Redemption, as it is written, "Behold, your king comes to you; you are victorious and triumphant, lowly, riding on a donkey."[338]

If you see yourself riding on a white donkey, happiness will soon befall you. Explanation: Either in regard to his wife or in regard to an inheritance.

If you see yourself plowing with a donkey, there will be a loss in your household.

If you see yourself riding on a king's donkey, you will be great.

If you see yourself riding on a donkey without a saddle blanket, you will be blessed. Others say: It signifies a loss.

If you see yourself riding on a donkey with a saddle, expect the Messiah.

If you see yourself falling from a donkey, it is a bad sign; others say: poverty.

If you see yourself eating donkey's meat, it is a bad sign; others say: poverty (R. Hai Gaon).

Horses:

All horses are good signs in dream, except for red ones.

If you see many horses in the month of Tishri, you will die at that time of the year (Daniel).

The Talmud states: Whoever sees a white horse in a dream, whether walking gently or galloping, it is a good sign; if a red horse, and walking gently, it is a good sign; if galloping, it is a bad sign.[339]

And in Sanhedrin chapter 10: "R. Papa said: We learn that a white horse is a good sign in a dream."[340]

If you see yourself chasing a horse and overtaking it, and then hitting the horse, you will be victorious over your enemies (R. Hai Gaon).

If you see yourself pulling a horse after you, you will follow the advice of great men. And R. Hai Gaon says: If with a bit, a great man will follow your advice.

If you see yourself riding a horse, and then it is stolen from you, you will lose your merchandise.

If you see yourself riding on a horse, greatness will be yours (R. Hai Gaon). Rashi adds: and good things. In *Sefer Zikhron Yaakov* I found: Whoever sees himself riding on a horse should expect the Redemption, as it is written: "That you are driving your steeds, your victorious chariots."[341] And in *Sefer Nefesh ha-Hayyim* it is written: "Whoever rides on a horse in a dream should rejoice, even if he is sad and worried about his child or his loss." This is because the word *sus,* "horse" is related to *sos,* "to rejoice" by the exchange of similar letters.[342]

If you see a horse galloping beneath you, and you fall from it, it is a sign of death. If you fall from it when it is at a walk, bemoan your sins (R. Hai Gaon). And Rashi wrote: If you see yourself falling from a horse, you will fall seriously ill. If you see yourself eating horse-meat, God is preparing your sustenance and your money will be protected.

Mule:

If you see yourself riding a mule, poverty will befall you (R. Hai Gaon). And Rashi wrote: Whoever rides a mule, trouble will come upon him.

If you see yourself falling off a mule, you will die at that time.

If you see yourself eating mule's flesh, you will accept money gained by illegal means.

If you ride on a king's mule, greatness will be yours.

She-mule:

If you see yourself riding on a she-mule, trouble will befall you.

If you see yourself falling off a she-mule, you will die at that time.

If you eat a she-mule's flesh, you will accept money obtained by illegal means.

Chapter Two
Wild Beasts

A. Harmful Ones

In gentile books it is stated that harmful wild beasts denote enemies.

Lion:

If you see a young lion, you will have a good year.

If you see yourself struggling with a lion and prevail, you will prevail over your enemies.

If you see a lion pursuing you, enemies will lie in wait and seek you.

If you see yourself joining with a lion, you will make peace with your enemies.

If you see a young lion before you, many of your enemies will start up with you. And if you see yourself leading one, you will prevail over your enemies. Alternatively: Your enemies will obey you.

If you see yourself riding on a lion, you will prevail over your enemies.

If you see yourself eating lion's flesh, you will be overtaken by great fear (R. Hai Gaon).

In the Talmud: Whoever sees a lion in a dream should rise early and recite the following verse, "The lion has roared, who will not fear?"[343] before another verse occurs to him, "A lion has gone up from his thicket."[344]

Bear:

If you see a bear pursuing an evil person, you will prevail over him (R. Hai Gaon).

If you see a bear attacking you, it signifies a dispute.

If you see a bear's head in your hand, you will obtain illegal wealth (R. Hai Gaon).

Wolf:

If you see a wolf, an enemy will soon arise against you.

Serpent:

[A Tanna recited before R. Sheshet:] Whoever sees a serpent, his sustenance is assured (Talmud)[345] (Others say: a good sign.) [The Talmud continues:] If it [i.e., the serpent] bites you, it [i.e., your sustenance] will be doubled.

(Others say: a bad sign. Still others say: Your enemies will increase.) If he kills, it, he will lose his sustenance. R. Sheshet said to him: All the more so will his sustenance be doubled! This is not so, however; R. Sheshet explained it this way because he actually saw a serpent in his dream and killed it. Explanation: It was for this reason that he interpreted the dream favorably. And the connection of the serpent with sustenance is because dust is to be found everywhere, and so the serpent's sustenance is commonly available to it, and it does not need to labor for it.[346] And if it bites him, this denotes that others will take his sustenance from him. On the other hand, this denotes that he will be wealthier than they, he the master and they the servants to do his bidding, and he will pay them for doing so. "If he kills it, his sustenance is lost." R. Sheshet, on the other hand, found a favorable explanation for this. While the serpent lived, it had to find its sustenance; this denotes that those who consume the master's wealth will be many, but when the serpent is killed, this denotes that the master will have a great deal of food available to him, since it was not consumed by his servants.

If you see a serpent fleeing from you, your sustenance is being diminished.

If you see a serpent sleeping or curled around your neck, sustenance will come to you.

If you see a serpent with its mate, wealth will come to you.

If you see a serpent in your lap, your sustenance is assured.

If you see a serpent in the water, and you have no wife, you will marry. If you have a wife, you will be widowed.

If you see yourself killing a serpent, it is a good sign and your enemies will fall before you (R. Hai Gaon).

Scorpion:

If you see yourself hunting a scorpion, you will be involved in a dispute.

Elephant:

[The Talmud states:] If you see an elephant in a dream, wonders will be performed for you.[347] But has it not been taught: All kinds of beasts are good signs in a dream, except an elephant and an ape? Elephants are a good sign if saddled, a bad one if not saddled.[348]

If you ride on an elephant in a dream, you will attain greatness.

B. Harmless wild beasts

Ram:

If you see a ram or pursue one, this foretells panic without pain (Daniel).

If you see yourself killing a ram, you will shed innocent blood.

If you see yourself riding a ram, you have committed a sin which has angered God.

If you see yourself given a ram as a gift, happiness and greatness will be yours (R. Hai Gaon).

Polecat:

If you see a polecat, you will have a good year.

If you eat a polecat's flesh, it signifies improved circumstances (R. Hai Gaon).

If you see a polecat, you will meet new people.

Beasts:

If you see desert beasts, it signifies trouble for nothing.

If you see bleating beasts, it signifies trouble and illness.

If you see yourself killed by evil beasts, lies will be told to you.

If you see wild beasts loping, it signifies dispute among the nations.

If you see yourself standing beside a wild beast, your relative is your enemy.

If you see a dead beast, your enemy is dead.

Cat:

If you see a cat in a dream, in a place where they call it a *shunara,* a beautiful song[349] will be composed for you; if in a place where they call it a *shinra,* you will undergo a change for the worse.[350] Explanation: the hint comes from the name, not from the thing itself. Therefore it seems to me that if one sees a cat in a dream nowadays, it is not to be interpreted by either of these solutions, since we no longer call a cat *shunara* or *shinra.* Rather, it is to be interpreted as R. Hai Gaon said: If you see a cat, you will merit stylish clothes, or according to the one who said that Heaven has decreed your death, but you have been saved from it.

Dogs:

If you see dogs running, you are the subject of gossip.

If you see yourself playing with dogs, your enemies will love you.

If you see dogs barking before you, your enemies' plan will succeed.

If you see a dog barking behind you, your enemies lie in wait for you.

If you see dogs pursuing you, it signifies governmental extortion (Daniel).

If you see that dogs have bitten you, your enemies will prevail against you.

If you see that you have led a dog, you will prevail over your enemies. If you straddle the dog, you will certainly prevail over your enemies. But if the dog straddles you, your enemies will prevail.

If you see yourself eating dog meat, you will move from place to place.

If you see yourself killing a dog, your enemy has been moved elsewhere.

The Talmud states: Whoever sees a dog in a dream should rise early and say, "But against any of the children of Israel no dog shall whet his tongue,"[351] before another verse occurs to him, "The dogs are greedy."[352]

Mouse:

If you see a mouse, you will meet someone new.

Deer:

If you kill a deer in a dream, you will spill innocent blood.

If you see yourself riding a deer, you have committed a sin which angers God.

If you see yourself given a deer as a gift, happiness and greatness will be yours (R. Hai Gaon).

Fox:

If you see a fox, you will fall ill. Others say: You will have a good year.

If you see yourself eating the flesh of a fox, it signifies improved circumstances (R. Hai Gaon).

Chapter Three
Birds

A. Ritually Clean Birds

[According to the Talmud:] All types of birds are good signs in a dream except for the owl, the horned owl, and the bat.[353]

Goose:

If you see a goose in your house, the honor of your house will increase.

If you see a goose, look forward to wisdom, as it is written: "Wisdom cries aloud in the street,"[354] and he who sees himself having intercourse with one will become head of the yeshiva. Said R. Ashi: I saw it and had intercourse with it [in the dream], and I attained greatness.[355]

Dove:

If you see yourself hunting a dove, you will have a daughter.

Birds:

If you see all sorts of birds fighting, you will be involved in a quarrel.

Bird:

If you see a bird, it is a good sign. Others say: There will be peace.

If you see a bird in your hand, good tidings will come to you.

If you see yourself catch a bird and it flees your hand, you must fast, as it is written, "As a bird wandering from its nest."[356]

If you see yourself eating a bird, it is a good sign.

If you see that a bird has bitten you, you have no need of anyone.

And in the Talmud: Whoever sees a bird will see peace. He should rise early and say: "Like a bird wandering from its nest."[357]

Turtledoves:

If you see turtledoves or young doves in a dream, and hunt one of them, you will have male children.

If you see yourself tying one of them, you will receive an inheritance. In gentile books: You will do a great deed.

If you see yourself eating the flesh of a turtledove, your luck will hold out.

Rooster:

[The Talmud says:] Whoever sees a rooster should look forward to male children.[358] Explanation: [The Hebrew word *tarnegol* (rooster) can be interpreted] as an acronym.[359] [Further explanation:] This is because no other living creature keeps as close to its mate as the rooster. Indeed, our Sages used the rooster as a symbol in this respect, for they advised scholars not to remain in the company of their wives as roosters do.[360] Thus, roosters represent children. Therefore it seems to me that dreaming of a capon, an emasculated rooster, indicates that one will not have children. Others [however, do not distinguish between capons and roosters, and] say that one will have children.

If you see a maidservant selling a rooster, you will merit children.

If you see roosters fighting, you will have a quarrel.

Hen:

[The Talmud says:] Whoever sees a hen should look forward to a garden pleasant and joyful.[361]

If you see many hens peregrinating in your house or in front of you, much wealth and honor will be yours (Rashi). Others say: If you see a hen, you will have nice living quarters.

B. Ritually Unclean Birds

Ostrich:

If you see yourself pursuing an ostrich but do not catch up to it, you will pursue wealth and not attain it.

If you see yourself riding an ostrich, you will attain greatness.

In gentile books it is written that the bird called *shiyuni* denotes a wise and righteous person, and that this is because it is white and pure, and seeks its food in the depths of the water, not stealing from others. At the end of its life it sings beautifully and dies. So too a righteous man whose life is pure and "white"— free from sin; he seeks knowledge and searches the depths for it; at the end of his life he teaches his wisdom and his secret knowledge to others—and dies.

The bird called "vulture" denotes a physician. This is because when this bird sees a wounded animal it tries with all its might to help it, even more so if it is red. For this reason it is easy to capture them by donning the skin of an apparently wounded animal. So too the physician, who tries to help the ill.

Bees:

If you see bees, your enemies will attack you.

Falcon or kite:

If you see a hawk or falcon above your house, you will take ill and recover.

If you see yourself hunting one of them, you will have a dispute with someone who trusts you.

If you see that he slaughtered one of them, it is a good sign.

If you eat of their flesh in a dream, good things will happen to you.

Flies:

If you see flies, it portends a robbery.

Hawk:

If you see yourself capturing a hawk, good things and honor will be yours.

Eagle:

If you see an eagle or a flying bird, you will attain greatness (Rashi). Others say: Greatness will be yours. And in the books of the gentiles it is written that the eagle denotes a king, and the falcon, a duke.

If you see yourself hunting an eagle, you will become wealthy; your enemies will fall before you.

If you see an eagle in your hand, it is a good sign.

If you slaughter an eagle, you will rule over people.

If you see yourself eating an eagle's flesh, you will be needed by people (R. Hai Gaon).

Ravens:

If you see ravens flying toward you, it is a good sign (Daniel); *Sefer Yosef ha-Tzaddik* says: you will find sustenance.[362]

If you see a raven on your head, you will die. If it is on someone else's head, that person will die. Proof of this is from the dream of Pharaoh's baker.[363]

Pelican:

If you see and hunt a pelican, you will fall ill and recover.

If you see a pelican on your house, you will have cause to mourn.

If you see yourself slaughtering a pelican or hear its sound but do not see it, it is a good sign.

If you eat of its flesh, you will have a financial loss.

If you see a pelican biting you or that you have lost one, good things and greatness will come to you.

If you see that you have slaughtered one, it portends a financial loss.

Owl:

If you see yourself slaughtering an owl, it portends a financial loss.

If you see and hunt an owl, you will take ill and recover.

If you see an owl over your house, you will have cause to mourn.

If you see yourself slaughtering an owl, or you hear its sound but do not see it, it is a good sign.

If you see yourself eating of its flesh, it portends a loss.

If you see that an owl has bitten you or that you have lost one, good things and greatness will be yours.

Chapter Four
Fish

Fish:

Fish denote coins with work, for their place is in the water, moving to and fro, and just as fish increase, so coins are the fruit of effort. Anyone who takes fish from people will take coins shamefully.

If you see your fish diminish, your money will diminish (Gentile books).

If you see fish, your enemies will attack you.

If you see yourself catching fish in a net, you will have children (*Daniel*). Others say: If you see fish, you will get a bad reputation.

If you see yourself catching fish with a hook or a net, God will give you a good life.

If you see yourself fishing for creeping things in the sea, it is a bad sign, except for what is called a dolphin and other agreeable creatures,[364] whether on sea or land (R. Hai Gaon). Rashi writes: If you see small fish, God will grant you improved circumstances; if they are big, He will grant you a great improvement.

If you see yourself fishing for fish, good tidings will come to you from elsewhere; others say: If you see yourself fishing for small fish, God will grant you a small present; if they are big, He will grant you improved circumstances and greatness.

Chapter Five
Animal Products

A. Dairy Products
Cheese:
If you eat fresh cheese, it signifies an improvement.
If you see yourself selling cheese, greatness will be yours.
Milk:
If you see milk, wealth and greatness will be yours, and your luck will improve.
If you see yourself selling milk, greatness will be yours.
Mother's milk:
If you see yourself nursing from full breasts, your situation will greatly improve (*Daniel*).
If you see yourself nursing from a woman's breasts, it signifies an improvement.
Mare's milk:
If you see yourself drinking mare's milk, you will find wealth.
Deer's milk:
If you drink deer or antelope milk, you will have a son and many good things.
Ewe's milk:
If you see yourself drinking ewe's milk, it signifies great improvement. Others say: You will have a small plan.
Different types of milk:
If you drink milk from various animals and it is sour, a bad sign (R. Hai Gaon).
If you drink milk from various animals and it is sweet, a good sign (R. Hai Gaon).
Milking:
If you see yourself milking sheep or goats, wealth will be yours.
Butter:
If you eat butter made from goat's milk, greatness will be yours.
If you eat butter, good tiding will come to you.

B. Eggs
Eggs:

All eggs are good signs, except ostrich eggs (Rashi).

[The Talmud says:] Whoever sees eggs in a dream, his request remains undecided.[365] Daniel says: His request will be fulfilled, his life will be lengthened, and he has merit.

If they are broken, your request will be granted. The same with nuts and cucumbers and glass containers and anything that can be broken open.[366] Explanation: Because an egg [*betzah* in Hebrew] is called *ba'ya* [in Aramaic, and *ba'ya* also means "want, desire"]. When one sees whole eggs, this denotes that one's request is undecided, just as the contents of the eggs are hidden from someone who wishes to eat them. If they are broken, his request is granted like this egg which has been broken, its contents are now revealed. The same goes for nuts, cucumbers, and everything which can be broken open.

If you see yourself seeking eggs, you will acquire menservants and maidservants.

If you see yourself eating boiled eggs, you will be saved from an illness which is about to befall you.

If you eat hardboiled eggs or scrambled eggs, know that your prayer has been accepted (R. Hai Gaon). Daniel says: Your request will be carried out. Others say: You will have a good life.

If you eat uncooked eggs, you will be in a good position.

If you eat hardboiled eggs in a deep frying pan, it is a bad sign.

C. Honey
Honey:

If you see honey mixed with bees, you will be surrounded by enemies.

If you see yourself tear a branch off a tree and use it to take honey, and then drink water, you will be saved from trouble (R. Hai Gaon).

Eating honey is a bad sign (*Daniel*).

If you see yourself eating honey, and it is good, it is a good sign; if bad, a bad sign (Rashi).

If you see yourself eating sweet honey, cooked and dried, illnesses will befall you.

If you see yourself eating a honey wafer, or any dish made with honey, it is a good sign.

Chapter Six
Meat

Blood:

If you see yourself eating blood, you will be saved from trouble.

Roast:

If you eat roast, trouble will bypass you (R. Hai Gaon).

Pot:

[The Talmud says:] R. Hanan said: There are three [kinds of dreams which symbolize] peace—a river, a bird, and a pot. . . . Whoever sees a pot in his dreams should rise early and say, "O Lord, You shall establish[367] peace for us,"[368] before another verse occurs to him, "Set it on the pot, set it on."[369]

Prepared food:

If you see yourself eating a dish, whether cooked or uncooked, and it is sour, it is a bad sign.

If you see yourself eating a salted or dried dish, serious illness will befall you. If it is without liquid but sweet, you will be happy.

If you see yourself eating from a plate and clean up whatever is in it, you have lost all your luck.

Gate Four
Men

Chapter One
Regarding Man Himself and Occurrences to His Body

Limbs:

The general significance of each limb is recorded in gentile books: the head, the kidneys, and the penis all represent the dreamer himself.

The shoulders represent wives and sisters, for we bear many things for wives and sisters, just as the shoulders bear a load.

The arms represent sons and daughters, for they are under our control.

The forearms represent friends, members of the household, and servants, for they help us, just as the forearm helps us.

The hand represents wise subordinates, for from them we receive perfect help, as from a hand.[370]

The testicles represent children.

The buttocks, feet, and lower legs represent sustenance of life.

The thighs represent relatives.

The intestines represent one's essential loves or wealth, which are as hidden and secret like one's intestines.

The liver and the blood represent one's treasure, for the blood denotes gold, since we often expend blood to obtain gold.

The Egyptians said that the liver represents desire and lust, blood represents anger, the heart represents the seat of life, skin diseases with blood or pus denote the essence [of the man] or gold. The hairs of the beard represent beauty and quiet, the hair on the arms represents women, pubic hair represents enemies, and the hair of other parts of the body represents wealth and beautiful golden vessels. Flying represents change of place or change of situation, depending on the context.

Cannibalism:
If you see yourself eating human flesh, you will hate a friend.

If you see yourself eating a human head, you will consume everything you have in illness.

Dumbness:
If you see yourself dumb, it is a good sign.

Testicles:
If you see one of your testicles fall, you will fall ill and recover (Rashi). Others say: You will lose a son.

Penis:
If you see a penis, you will have a son.

If you see an erect penis, it foretells the strength of sons.

If you see your penis cut off, you will die that year (Rashi). Others say: If your penis is cut off, your descendants will be cut off.

Nipples:
If you see your nipples cut off, it is a sign of trouble (Rashi).

Blood:
If you see blood issuing from your body but do not writhe in pain, your sins are being brought to Heaven's attention. Others say: They are being taken away.

If you see your penis urinating blood, your wife will miscarry.

Beard:
If you see your beard ripped out, you will gain an evil reputation (R. Hai Gaon). Others say: If you see your beard plucked out or falling, it portends trouble.

Forearms:
If you see your forearms smooth and white, great men will love you (R. Hai Gaon).

If you see your forearms ugly or dirty, your friends will tell lies about you (R. Hai Gaon).

If you see your forearms fallen off the body, an evil time will befall you (R. Hai Gaon).

Group:
If you see yourself joining a group, the anger of others will depart from you.

Illness:
If you see yourself ill, you will rejoice during that year.

Purity:
If you see yourself become ritually pure, it is a bad sign.

Your hands:
If you see your hands cut off, you will not need the use of your hands (R. Hai Gaon).[371]

Barefoot:
If you see yourself barefoot, it portends a loss.

Sleeping:
If you dream you are asleep, it is a good sign.

Jawbone:
If you see your jaws fallen off, those who advocate evil against you will die.

Your intestines:
If you see your intestines come out, you will bury your children (Rashi).

Parapet:
If you see yourself falling from the parapet of your house, it means trouble.

Forehead:
If you see your forehead broken, it means trouble.

Bloodletter:
[The Talmud states:] A Tanna recited before R. Nahman [b. Isaac]: [If he dreams that he is undergoing] bloodletting,[372] his sins are forgiven. But has it not been taught [elsewhere]: His sins are laid out? What is meant by "laid out"? Laid out to be forgiven.[373] Explanation: Since sins are described as red, as it is stated: "If your sins are red as crimson."[374]

But R. Hai Gaon says: [If someone dreams that he is undergoing bloodletting] from the nose, his days will be shortened. If from the shoulders, he will lose something important. If from the forearms, a small loss will come to him.

If you see yourself undergoing a major bloodletting, it is a good sign.

Judgment:
If you see yourself undergoing judgment and are saved, it portends trouble.

Death:
If you see yourself die in a dream, it is a good sign.

Nostrils:
If you see your nose bleeding, you will take ill and recover. If you are covered with blood, it signifies a financial loss (R. Hai Gaon). Explanation: Blood represents money. And therefore, "if you see that blood coming out of your nostrils," it is a sign that money which you earned by the sweat of your brow[375] will be spent to cure illnesses. And they said that he will recover because blood from the nose signifies recovery. "If he is covered with blood, it indicates a financial loss"—this means that he would not have recovered without incurring these expenses.

Eye:

If you have pain in your eye, it is a bad sign.

Excrement:

Excrement from a sick person or from someone else represents money earned in an evil way. Just as excrement is hidden but becomes known with intestinal problems, so too money earned in an evil way.

And in the Talmud: If he dreams that he is moving his bowels, it is a good sign for him, as it is written: "He that is bent down shall speedily be let free."[376] But this is only if he did not wipe himself in his dream.[377]

Another version: Your needs are being met, as it is written, "He that is bent down shall speedily be let free."[378] This applies only if he did not wipe himself. Explanation: One who moves his bowels removes the poison from himself, and that is why it is a good sign. As for the alternative version, "His needs are met, so long as he does not wipe himself"—so that his hands do not become unclean. This is a sign that you will need to dirty your hands in order to fulfill your needs and with the sweat of your brow you will eat bread.[379]

Nails:

If you see your fingernail torn and bad looking, it is a sign of wisdom (Rashi).

Height:

If you see your height increase, you will live many years.

Head:

If you see yourself washing your head, you will be saved from every trouble.

Riding:

If you see yourself riding on another man's neck, you will ride on the necks of your adversaries [i.e., you will defeat them.]

Running:

If you see yourself running in a dream, it is a good sign.

Feet:

If you see yourself with your feet cut off, you will go to a far-off place.

If you see one of your haunches cut off, you will fall ill and recover.

Teeth:

If you see your teeth grown long, it is a good sign. And Rashi says that great redemption will come.

If you see your molars fall out, your daughters or sisters will die (R. Hai Gaon).

If you see a tooth sprout in a dream, it signifies illness.

If you see a black tooth, trouble will soon come.

If you see a loose tooth in a dream, it signifies illness.

If you see a loose tooth in a dream and it then falls out, it foretells death. And for this reason it has become customary to fast for your dream, even on a Sabbath.[380] Many say that if the tooth causes pain as it falls out, it is a sign that the person will die and his death will be very painful. But if it does not cause pain as it falls out, it is a sign that the person will die painlessly.

Hair:

If you see yourself shaving with a razor in a dream, and have only very short hairs on your head, like a "crewcut," it is a good sign.

Urine:

Urine denotes many things, depending on the context. For example, if you see urine in a silver or golden vessel or in something expensive, it indicates that you will have children with a noblewoman (gentile books).

If you see urine in a ugly vessel, it indicates an ugly woman (gentile books).

Shaving:

The Talmud states: If you shave your head in a dream, it is a good sign for you; if your head and your beard, it is a good sign for you and your whole family.[381]

If you dream about shaving, rise early and say, "And Joseph shaved himself and changed his garments,"[382] before another verse occurs to you, "If I be shaven, then my strength will depart from me."[383]

Hanging:

If you see yourself hanging, you will ascend to greatness; and if you descend head-first, do not fear, for though your time is delayed, you will repent [and all will be well].

Fasting:

If you see yourself fasting, it is a bad sign. In the Talmud [it is stated: R. Hisda said:] Any dream but one about a fast.[384] Explanation: Any dream [may be favorable] except one in which you see yourself fasting. And for this reason people have become accustomed to fasting for such a dream even on the Sabbath.[385] Others say: this is particularly the case at the time of the Neilah prayer on Yom Kippur; the reason seems to be that if one has such a dream at that time, [when Yom Kippur is nearly over and one's sins have presumably been forgiven], it indicates that he still has sins to atone for and therefore still must fast, and so it is a bad sign.

Chapter Two
Regarding Kings and Nobles

Wise men:
The Talmud states: There are three Sages whose presence in a dream is meaningful: R. Akiva,[386] let the dreamer look forward to wisdom; R. Eleazar b. Azariah, let him look forward to greatness and wealth;[387] R. Ishmael b. Elisha, let him fear punishment.[388] Explanation: R. Ishmael was one of the ten Sages killed by the Romans, who stripped the skin off his face before he died.

The Talmud continues: There are three disciples of the Sages whose presence in a dream is meaningful: Ben Azai, let him look forward to piety; Ben Zoma, let him look forward to wisdom;[389] "The Other One,"[390] says: let him fear punishment. Explanation: He will be punished in Gehenna.[391]

If you see Ishmael son of Abraham,[392] yours prayer will be heard. Explanation: As the Torah says: "For the Lord has heard the voice of the lad."[393]

If you see Pinhas, a wonder will be performed for you.[394] Explanation: Just as a miracle was performed for Pinhas, as explained in tractate Sanhedrin.[395]

If you see R. Huna, a wonder will be performed for you.[396] If you see Hanina, Hananiah, or Jonathan, wonders will be performed for you.[397] This refers to seeing the names in written form.

And in the Zohar, Parashat Vayishlah:[398] Said R. Yasa: I have heard that whoever has a dream and sees Jacob adorned in his clothes, life will be added to his years.

King:
If you see a king in a dream, you will attain greatness (R. Hai Gaon).

If you see yourself speaking with a king, and he greets you, the king loves you; if you are angry, he hates you (R. Hai Gaon).

If you see the king forced from his throne, there will be a great anger against this land (R. Hai Gaon).

The Talmud states: There are three kings whose appearance in a dream is meaningful: One who sees David in a dream may look forward to piety; Solomon, he may look forward to wisdom; Ahab,[399] let him fear punishment.[400]

Slave:

If you see a slave in a dream, it is a bad sign.

A person's name:

If you see a person in a dream whose name has the letter *shin* in it, it is a bad sign, except for King Saul.

If you see a person whose name has the letter *nun*, it is as if you were seeing the Divine Presence. Joseph the Righteous[401] says that this refers to one that has two *nuns*, as in the combined name Jonathan Yohanan.

If you see a person whose name begins with *yod*, it is a bad sign.

Nobles:

Seeing nobles in a dream is a very good omen.

Maidservant:

If you see a maidservant, it is a good sign.

Chapter Three
Regarding Intercourse with Women

A woman:

If you see a woman clapping her hands in sorrow or dancing, it foretells an incident of fornication.

Intercourse:

In general, according to gentile books, sleeping with a married woman in a dream denotes success and profit. However, sleeping with a virgin denotes vain effort, for virgins are generally still unable to conceive. For this reason, a prostitute's adornment denotes an improvement in your circumstances, and of sterile women denotes harm.

The Talmud states: If you dream that you are committing incest with your mother, look forward to obtaining understanding.[402] R. Hai Gaon says that this denotes that you will live a good life and may look forward to obtaining understanding.

If you dream that you are committing incest with your sister, look forward to wisdom, as it says: "Say to wisdom, 'You are my sister.'"[403]

Likewise, the Talmud states: Whoever dreams that he has committed adultery with a married woman may be assured that he has a portion in the world to come; this refers to a case in which he does not know her and did not think about her the evening before.[404] This condition [not knowing her] seems to apply to all such dreams.

The explanation for the fact that these sinful acts are actually good signs is that intercourse is considered one-sixtieth of the pleasure of the Garden of Eden [i.e., the world to come], and illegitimate intercourse is all the more so, as it states, "Stolen waters are sweet."[405] Moreover, it hints that he will receive a double portion, his own and the woman's husband's portion, in the Garden of Eden, which is compared to a wife. However, the *Book of Sefer Yosef ha-Tzaddik* states: If you lie with a married woman in a dream, it is a sign of dispute. Others say; Whoever commits adultery with a married woman will become the head of a court.

The Talmud says: Whoever has intercourse with a betrothed maiden may look forward to knowledge of Torah, as it states, "Moses commanded us a Torah, an inheritance of the congregation of Jacob."[406] Read *me'orashah,* "betrothed," rather than *morashah,* "an inheritance."[407]

Virgin:

If you see a virgin in a dream, it is a sign of contentment (but see above).

A woman's nipples:

If you see a woman's nipples, it is a sign of wealth.

A wedding canopy:

If you see a wedding canopy, whether over yourself or someone else, it is a bad omen.

A birthing woman:

If you see a woman giving birth, one of your relatives will die. So, too, if you see a woman giving birth suddenly.

A bed:

If you see a made bed, it is a good sign.

Intercourse:

If you lie with a male, evil times will befall you.

If you lie with a virgin, it is a good sign (*Daniel*). Others say: Serious illness will befall you.

If you lie with a woman by chance and you love her, it is a good sign (*Daniel*).

If you lie with a menstruant woman, it is a bad sign.

If you lie with a prostitute, it signifies that improved circumstances, salvation, and money will come to you.

If you lie with a widow or divorced woman whom you love, it is a good sign.

A woman's hair:

If you see yourself with a woman's hair on you, ugly things will be said about you.

Chapter Four
Regarding the Dead

A coffin:

If you see yourself in a coffin and grave, troubles will befall you, but perhaps you will be saved (R. Hai Gaon).

A cemetery:

If you see yourself staying in a cemetery overnight, you will spend a night in jail.

A murderer:

If you see yourself kill someone, a miracle will be performed for you.

A eulogy:

The Talmud states: Whoever dreams about a eulogy, they will have mercy on him in Heaven and will redeem him. This refers to a written eulogy.

The Angel of Death:

If you speak to the Angel of Death in a dream, you will fall ill and recover. But if you are on his head, you will die. If you are at his feet,[408] you will fall ill to the point of death and recover.

The dead:

If you see yourself dead, you have done something for which God will bring you close to Him. Daniel says: Life will be added to your years.

And in the Talmud: Our Rabbis taught: Whoever dreams about a corpse in the house, it is a good sign for the house.[409] If it was eating and drinking in the house, it is a good sign for the entire household.[410] If it took clothing from the house, it is a bad sign for the house. R. Papa explained this to refer to a shoe or a sandal. Whatever a dead person takes from the house is a good sign except a shoe and a sandal; anything that it puts down is a good sign except dust and mustard.[411] The explanation: When it takes shoes and sandals, that is a sign that the members of the household will go barefoot or will cease going to the marketplace. Likewise, dust is a sign of burial, as is mustard, which is as fine as dust.

If you see dead bodies in a dream, and you are healthy, have no fear at all; but if you are ill, it is a bad sign.

If you see yourself speaking with the dead, remain in the company of good people and do as they do.

If you see a dead relative coming to see you, you will be wealthy. If the dead man embraces you or kisses you, and even more, if he bites you, trouble will befall you.

If you see a corpse give you something, it indicates improved circumstances. But if the object is something which begins with the letter *nun* or *lamed*, you will become poor (R. Hai Gaon).

If the dead person gives the living one an iron implement or a weapon, he should feel secure no matter where he goes (R. Hai Gaon). And Rashi says: If the dead person gave him something which he did not want to take from him, it is a bad sign.

If you see your deceased father and mother, a joyful occasion will be yours. If they give you something, all the more so.

If you see yourself washing a dead body or dressing it or carrying it, you will descend from your high status.

If you follow a coffin or console the mourners, you will have performed a deed for which God will bring you close to Him (R. Hai Gaon).

If you see the dead robbing the living, one of your relatives will die.

Burial:

If you see yourself buried, you will be given over into the power of a cruel person.

Graves:

If you see graves, it foretells ugly deeds.

Burial clothes:

If you see burial clothes in a dream, you have performed a deed for which God will bring you close to Him.

Chapter Five
Clothes

Clothing generally denotes beauty, honor, and usefulness (gentile books). Others say: If you see yourself wearing costly clothes, you will attain greatness; if you take them off, you will lose your position.

If you remove golden garments from their storage place, it is a very good sign.

Lost:

If you dream that you have lost your clothes, it signifies a loss.

A woman in a man's clothes:

If you see your wife wearing your clothes, she will inherit you (R. Hai Gaon).

Clothes:

If you see yourself belted in silk, you will attain greatness (R. Hai Gaon).

If you see yourself dressed in silk, people will be jealous of you.

If you see yourself wearing gold or silver, you will attain greatness never before conceived (R. Hai Gaon).

Black clothes:

If you see black clothes or any color, you will have troubles.

A prayer shawl:

If you see yourself wearing a new prayer shawl, you will marry (R. Hai Gaon).

A royal crown:

If you see a royal crown on your head, good fortune will soon come to you.

If you see a crown or turban taken off your head, your luck will decrease.

A woman's clothes:

If you see a woman's dress, you have committed a sin (R. Hai Gaon).

Colors:

The Talmud states: All colors are good in a dream except blue.[412] Explanation: Blue is close to green, and one whose face is green is ill.

If you wear red clothes in a dream, trouble will befall you; you will be punished. If you wear white, it is a sign of good deeds, as it is written, "If your

114

sins are as crimson, they will become white as snow"[413] (Rashi). Daniel says: If you see yourself dressed in white, it foretells a time of good tidings; explanation: the opposite of red. Black, a bad sign.

Torn clothes:

If you see your clothes torn in a dream, the heavenly decree regarding you has been torn up.[414]

Burned clothes:

If you see your clothes suddenly burn up, you will profit. That is to say: suits of clothing will be made up for you, for just as the fire burns quickly, etc.

Nakedness:

If you see yourself naked, it signifies shame or trouble (R. Hai Gaon). But *Sefer Yosef ha-Tzaddik* says: poverty.

In the Talmud: If you see yourself naked outside the Land of Israel,[415] you will remain sinless; if in the Land of Israel, you will be bereft of mitzvot.[416] Explanation: This depends on another statement of our Sages: Whoever resides outside the Land of Israel is as one who has no God, as it is written, "They have driven me out this day [that I should not cleave to the inheritance of the Lord, saying: Go, serve other gods."[417] Now, whoever said to David, "Serve other gods"? Rather, whoever lives outside the Land of Israel is as one who worships idols.][418] This being so, anyone who remains outside the Land remains in a sinful state—and therefore one who is naked is sinless, [while the reverse is true when one stands naked in the Land of Israel]. He who stands in the Land of Israel is as full of mitzvot as a pomegranate is full of seeds—and one who is naked lacks these, and so is full of sin.

Undressing:

If you see yourself undressing, and you are ill, it is a good sign.

Sewing:

If you see yourself sewing a garment, it denotes legal decision-making. Others say: it foretells building a house. Explanation: Just as a tailor joins piece to piece, so a scholar who renders a decision joins and ties statements and laws together to determine the decision; the other interpretation likens the joining of pieces of cloth to the joining of stones to construct a house.

Gate Five
Heavenly Bodies

Chapter One
Sun, Moon, and Stars

Moon:

The moon denotes rulership. Therefore, if you see the moon eclipsed in a dream, it denotes death or illness (gentile books).

If you see the moon over[419] the land, things will be well for you (Rashi).

If you see the moon eclipsed in a dream, there will be anger against the entire province (Rashi).

Stars:

Stars denote brothers, friends, teachers, or nations (gentile books). Others say: If you see stars, it foretells improved circumstances. Still others: If you see stars arranged in groups, you will receive good tidings, for the king and the army are in your power.[420]

If you see stars falling from the sky, a great host will die in war (Rashi).

If you see stars quenched, flee from disputes.

Heavens:

If you see yourself ascend higher than the heavens, your province will have hard times due to the king's doings (Rashi).

If you see the heavens covered with clouds, something important will be lost.

Sun:

The sun denotes a king, father, rulership. Therefore, if you see an eclipse in a dream, it denotes either death or illness.

If you see the sun over[421] the land, it is a good sign.

If you see the sun in eclipse in a dream, there will be anger against the entire province (Rashi).

If you see the heavens falling, it foretells a great fall (R. Hai Gaon).

If you see the sun in two places in the heavens, there will be a new ruler in your city (R. Hai Gaon).

If you see the sun quenched, flee disputes.

If you see the sun blacken, the king will die and there will be a dispute.

Chapter Two
Thunder

Thunder and lightning:

If you see thunder and lightning without rain, your generation is sinful and God is angry with them (Rashi).

If you see thunder and lightning and rain altogether, it signifies a good time for your province (Rashi).

Rain:

If you see violent rain descending unseasonably, an evil decree will be issued against your city.

Chapter Three
Books

A letter:

If you see a new letter, it is a good sign.

The letter *tet*:

The Talmud states: Said R. Joshua b. Levi: If you see the letter *tet* in a dream, it is a good sign for you. Why? Said R. Asi: Because the Torah opens with goodness first, as it states: "The Lord saw that the light was good."[422] Explanation: The word "good" [Hebrew: *tov*] is the first word in the Torah employing the letter *tet*.

Amen:

The Talmud states: If you see yourself answering "Amen, may His great Name be blessed," be assured that you have a portion in the world to come.[423]

Hazzan:

If you see that you are a hazzan,[424] and you are worthy of the post, greatness will be yours; but if not, degradation.

Schoolteacher:

If you see yourself as a schoolteacher,[425] you will be a ranking official.

Books of Scripture:

Three books of Prophets[426] are meaningful in dreams:

If you see the Book of Kings, look forward to piety.

If you see the Book of Isaiah, look forward to wisdom.

If you see the Book of Jeremiah, expect punishment.[427]

Three books of Writings[428] are meaningful in dreams:

If you see the Book of Psalms, look forward to piety.

If you see the Book of Proverbs, look forward to wisdom.

If you see the Book of Job, expect suffering.

Three minor books are meaningful in dreams:

If you see the Song of Songs, look forward to piety.[429]

If you see the Book of Kohelet, look forward to wisdom.[430]

If you see the Book of Esther, a miracle will be performed for you.[431]

A sefer Torah:[432]

People generally believe that seeing a Torah scroll burned in a dream is a bad sign. Others say: Seeing a Torah scroll without its wrappings or reading from a Torah scroll. This is taken so seriously that one who dreams of this fasts on that day, even if it is a Sabbath.[433] Women say that seeing a Torah scroll treated honorably foretells the birth of a son.

The Shema:

If you see yourself reciting the Shema, you are worthy of having the Divine Presence rest on you, just as Moses was,[434] but your generation is not worthy of it happening.[435]

Rosh Hashanah:

If you see that it is Rosh Hashanah, and you are blowing the ram's horn, fast and beg for mercy, for your sins are hanging about you.[436]

Tefillin:

If you see yourself putting on tefillin, look forward to greatness, as it is written, "And all the peoples of the earth shall see that the name of the Lord is called upon you, and they shall fear you,"[437] and R. Eliezer the Great says: This refers to the tefillin of the head.

Thus ends my collection of dream interpretations, that I have gleaned with great labor.

And now I will come to my second point. It is impossible to mention everything that may be seen in dreams, but these above are the essential categories. From them the interpreter may compare and analogize and so interpret what is dreamed. Moreover, it is clear that all the details of the interpretations presented here are really dependent on the time, place, and situation of the dreamer, and the circumstances of the vision, all according to the characteristics and conjectures I have presented above.

Furthermore, the interpretations mentioned above all refer only to the simplest understanding of what a person dreams. In actuality, the would-be interpreter must distinguish between similar visions and use his own understanding in order to understand the combinations of the elements described above, as they occur in a dream.

The correct procedure is to isolate the important elements in their proper light, both from what is recorded in books and from one's own understanding or conjecture, eliminating the unimportant elements. Then one must determine what each important element portends in order to build up a complete picture of the matter and event which is foretold. In order to make the process understandable, I will cite several examples of dreams that were dreamed in the past and then came to pass.

Joseph dreamed two dreams, one about the sheaves and one about the stars, and Pharaoh also dreamed two, one about the cows and one about the sheaves.

Pharaoh's Chief Cupbearer and Chief Baker likewise dreamed two dreams, one each, in the same night.[438] [Each of these dreams included a multitude of details, and Joseph's wisdom consisted, in part, of isolating the important from the unimportant.]

Thus, the Chief Cupbearer saw a vine on which there were three branches, and as it budded its clusters ripened into grapes; he took the grapes, squeezed them into a cup, and put it in Pharaoh's hand.[439] Joseph interpreted the three branches as representing three days—"in three days Pharaoh will pardon you and restore you to your post; place Pharaoh's cup in his hand as was your custom formerly when you were his cupbearer."[440] Similarly, the Chief Baker saw three baskets on his head, one above the other, and in the uppermost basket there were all kinds of foods for Pharaoh that a baker prepares; and the birds were eating out of the basket on his head.[441] Joseph interpreted the baskets as likewise representing three days—"in three days Pharaoh will lift off your head and impale you on a pole."[442] And, as we know, his interpretations were fulfilled.

Note the wisdom of Joseph's interpretations, for even though it may seem that the two dreams were identical, Joseph distinguished between them, as we explained in Part One, Gate Six.[443] He understood that the Chief Cupbearer's dream meant that in three days he would return to his post while the Chief Baker would be impaled. In particular, the sight of the vine indicated that the Cupbearer would soon return to pouring wine, as the vine in the dream grew in order that wine should issue from it. Joseph then interpreted the dream as indicating three periods of time, corresponding to the three branches, but he did not yet know the length of time, whether years or months. So he interpreted the speed of the budding as indicating the speed of the Cupbearer's return. This was because, as is well known, a vine goes through three stages of growth: buds, immature grapes, and mature grapes. Since the verse skipped the middle stage, and proceeded directly from buds to grapes, speed was indicated. The periods of time indicated by the branches must therefore be days—after three days the Cupbearer would return to his post.

However, the Chief Baker's dream denoted the reverse of the Chief Cupbearer's. First of all, he did not see Pharaoh in his dream. Moreover, though the bird ate from the basket on his head, he did not feed it; and for this reason Joseph interpreted the three baskets as referring to three days—the fact that the food was only in one basket [indicated the shortness of the time period]. [Since the bird ate from the third basket, this] indicated that on the third day the jailers would come and impale him, with the food on him in order to publicize his crime; the birds would then eat his flesh.

In the Book of Judges, when Gideon was about to do battle with Midian, one of the Midianites dreamed that a loaf of barley bread from the Israelite camp was whirling through the Midianite camp; it struck a tent and knocked it down.[444] The Midianites interpreted this as follows: "It can only mean the sword of the Israelite Gideon son of Joash. God is delivering Midian and the entire camp into his hands."[445] And so it was; the loaf of barley bread represented people [i.e., the Israelites] who were sustained by bread, and with the strength it provided they quickly fell upon the Midianite camp, attacking and defeating it.

[R. Almoli now recounts dreams from various sources, including, it would seem, his own experience, that illustrate the symbolism described in the preceding chapters.]

And in the Talmud:[446] Bar Hadaya was an interpreter of dreams. He gave favorable interpretations to those who paid him, and unfavorable interpretations to those who did not. Abaye and Rava each had a dream. Abaye gave him a zuz, and Rava did not give him anything.

They said to him: In our dream we had to read the verse "Your ox will be slain before your eyes."[447] To Rava he said: Your business will fail, and you will be so unhappy that you will lose your appetite. To Abaye he said: Your business will prosper, and you will be unable to eat from joy.

They then said to him: In our dream we had to read the verse "You shall beget sons and daughters but they shall not be yours."[448] For Rava he interpreted this dream unfavorably; to Abaye he said: You will have many sons and daughters, and your daughters will be married and go away, making it seem to you that they have been taken captive.

Again, they said to him: We were made to read the verse "Your sons and daughters will be given to another people."[449] To Abaye he said: You will have many sons and daughters; you will want your daughters to marry your relatives, and your wife will want them to marry her relatives. In the end she will force you to marry them to her relatives, which will be like giving them to another people. To Rava he said: Your wife will die, and her sons and daughters will come under the rule of another wife. (For Rava said in the name of R. Jeremiah b. Abba, in the name of Rav: What is the meaning of the verse "Your sons and daughters will be given to another people"?[450] This refers to a stepmother.)

Again: We were made to read the verse "Go your way, eat your bread with joy, etc."[451] To Abaye he said: Your business will prosper, and you will eat and drink, reciting this verse out of joy. To Rava he said: Your business will fail, you will slaughter cattle and not eat or drink, and you will read verses in order to assuage your worry.

Again: We were made to read the verse "You shall carry much seed out into the field, and gather little in, for the locusts will consume it."[452] For Abaye he interpreted from the first favorable half of the verse; to Rava from the second unfavorable part.

Again: We were made to read the verse "And all the peoples of the earth shall see that the name of the Lord is called upon you, etc."[453] To Abaye he said: Your name will be famous as the head of the yeshiva, and you will be generally held in awe. To Rava he said: The king's treasury will be broken into, and you will be arrested as a thief, and everyone will hold you up as a negative example—["If this can happen to Rava, how much more so to me!"]. The next day the king's treasury was broken into and they came and arrested Rava.

Abaye and Rava said to Bar Hadaya: We saw a lettuce on the mouth of a jar. To Abaye he said: Your business will be doubled like lettuce; to Rava he said: Your business will be bitter as lettuce.

They said to him: We saw some meat on the mouth of a jar. To Abaye he said: Your wine will be sweet and everyone will come to buy meat and wine from you; to Rava he said: Your wine will turn sour and everyone will go to buy meat to eat with it [i.e., to use it as a dip—hardly worth the trouble to sell].

They said to him: We saw a cask hanging from a palm tree. To Abaye he said: Your business will spring up like a palm tree; to Rava he said: Your goods will be sweet like dates [i.e., cheap, and no great profit will be made from them].

They said to him: We saw a pomegranate sprouting from the mouth of a jar. To Abaye he said: Your goods will be high-priced like a pomegranate; to Rava he said: Your goods will be stale like a dry pomegranate.

They said to him: We saw a cask fall into a pit. To Abaye he said: Your goods will be in demand, as people say: The pu'ah (a medicine) has fallen into the well and cannot be found [but all seek it]. To Rava he said: Your goods will be spoiled and thrown into a pit.

They said: We saw a young donkey standing by our pillow and braying. To Abaye he said: You will become a king [i.e., head of the yeshiva], and a spokesman will stand by you [to repeat your lectures out loud]. To Rava he said: The words "firstborn of a donkey"[454] which appear on the parchment in the tefillin has been erased from your tefillin. Rava said to him: I have looked at them and they are there. He answered him: Certainly the vav of the word hamor [donkey] has been erased from your tefillin. [Rava examined his tefillin and found that the vav of hamor had been erased.] Subsequently Rava went by himself and said to him: I dreamed that the outer door fell down. He said to him: Your wife will die. He said to him: I dreamed that my front and back teeth fell out. He said to him: Your sons and daughters will die. He said: I saw two pigeons flying. He said: You will divorce two wives.[455] He said to him: I saw two turnip-tops. He replied: You will receive two blows with a club which resembles a turnip-top. On that day Rava went and sat all day in the House of Study. He found two blind men quarreling with one another. Rava went to separate them and they gave him two blows. They wanted to give him another blow but he said: Enough! In my dream I only saw two!

Finally Rava went and paid his [i.e., Bar Hadaya's] fee. He said to him: I saw a wall fall down. He replied: You will acquire wealth without end. He said: I dreamed that Abaye's house fell in and the dust of it covered me. He answered him: Abaye will die and the leadership of his yeshiva will be offered to you. He said to him: I saw my own house fall in, and everyone came and took a brick. He said to him: Your teachings will be disseminated throughout the world. He said to him: I dreamed that my head was split open and my brains fell out. He answered; The stuffing will fall out of your pillow. He said to him: In my dream I was made to read the Hallel in praise of the Exodus from Egypt. He answered: Miracles will happen to you.

Bar Hadaya was once traveling with Rava on a boat. He said to himself: Why should I accompany a man to whom a miracle will happen?[456] As he left the boat, he dropped a book; Rava found it, and saw written in it: All dreams follow the mouth [i.e., the interpretation]. He exclaimed: It all depended on you, and you gave me all this pain! I forgive you everything except what you said about the daughter of R. Hisda [i.e., Rava's wife, whose death Bar Hadaya foretold]. May it be God's will that you be handed over to the government, and that they have no mercy on you. Bar Hadaya said to himself: What should I do? We have been taught that a curse uttered by a Sage, even when undeserved, is fulfilled; how much more so does this hold for Rava, whose curse was deserved! He thought: I will go into exile, for it has been taught: Exile atones for sin. He fled to the Romans. The keeper of the emperor's wardrobe had a dream, and said to him: I dreamed that a needle pierced my finger; what does it mean? Bar Hadaya said to him: Give me a zuz [and I will interpret it for you]. The keeper refused to pay, and he would not say a word to him. The keeper again said to him: I dreamed that a worm fell between two of my fingers. He said to him: Give me a zuz. He refused to pay, and he would not say a word to him. The keeper again said to him: I dreamed that a worm filled the whole of my hand. He said to him: Worms have been spoiling all the silk garments. This became known in the palace, and they brought out the keeper of the wardrobe in order to put him to death. He said to them: Why execute me? Bring the man who knew and would not tell. They brought Bar Hadaya and said to him: Because of your zuz, the king's silken garments have been ruined.

They tied two cedars together with a rope, tied one of his legs to one cedar and the other to the other, and let the rope go so that even his head was split. Each tree rebounded to its place, and he was decapitated and his body fell in two.

Ben Dama, the son of R. Ishmael's sister, asked R. Ishmael: I dreamed that both my jaws fell out; what does it mean? R. Ishmael answered: Two Roman leaders were plotting against you, but they have died.

Bar Kappara said to Rabbi Judah the Prince: I dreamed that my nose (*af*) fell off; what does it mean? He answered: Fierce anger (*af*) has been removed from you. He said to him: I dreamed that both my hands were cut off; what does it mean? He answered: You will not need your hands to work. He said to him: I dreamed that both my legs were cut off; what does it mean? He answered: You will ride on horseback. I dreamed that they said to me: You will die in Adar and not see Nisan; what does it mean? He answered: You will die in all honor (*adruta*) and not be brought into temptation (*nisayon*).

A certain heretic said to R. Ishmael: I saw myself in a dream pouring oil on olives. He answered: You have slept with your mother. (Explanation: olive oil is the product of the olive, and so represents the son; "pouring oil" on his mother therefore represents intercourse.) He said to him: I dreamed I plucked a star. He answered: You have kidnapped an Israelite [who is compared to a star].[457] He said to him: I dreamed that I swallowed a star.[458] He said to him: You have sold an Israelite and consumed the proceeds. He said to him: I dreamed that my eyes were kissing one another. He answered: You have slept with your sister. He said to him: I dreamed that I kissed the moon. He answered: You slept with the wife of an Israelite. He said to him: I dreamed that I was walking in the shade of a myrtle. He answered: You have slept with someone else's betrothed. He said to him: I dreamed that there was shade above me and beneath me. He answered: It refers to unnatural intercourse. He said to him: I saw ravens continually coming on to my bed. He answered: Your wife has committed adultery with many men. He said to him: I saw doves continually coming to my bed. He answered: You have defiled many women. He said to him: I dreamed that I took two doves and they flew away. He answered: You have married two wives and divorced them without a divorce document. He said to him: I dreamed that I was shelling eggs. He answered: You have been stripping the dead. He then said to him: You are right about everything but the last. Just then a woman came and said to him: The cloak you are wearing belonged to So-and-So who is dead, and you have stripped it from him. He said to him: I dreamed that people told me: Your father left you money in Cappadocia. He said to him: Have you money in Cappadocia? He answered, No. Did your father ever go to Cappadocia? No. In that case, he said, *kappa* means a beam in Aramaic and *dika* means ten in Greek. Go and examine the first beam of ten, for it is full of coins. He went, and found it full of coins. . . .

NOTE: The following appendices are not by R. Almoli, but may be of interest to readers.

Appendix One

In which the categories of dreams and their nature are explained from the work *Nishmat Hayyim* by Rabbi Manasseh ben Israel.

Dreams can be divided into three categories, each more exalted than the other. These are: prophetic dreams, providential dreams, and natural dreams.

A natural dream comes to a person by reason of his predominant temperament or condition.[459] That is, when a certain natural heat or unnatural fever grows, the person dreams that he is warming himself by a fire or is in a warm bath, etc. And, conversely, when his body cools down, he dreams of snow, rain, or similar cold objects. Dreams of this kind are vain, they have no reality, and it was regarding them that Isaiah said, "as though a hungry man dreams that he is eating, but upon wakening his soul is empty, or as though a thirsty man dreams that he is drinking, but upon wakening he is faint and his soul is parched."[460] Likewise, in Zechariah, "the *teraphim* speak delusion . . . and dreams speak vanity,"[461] and as our Sages, may their memory be for a blessing, said, "Dreams have no effect in legal matters."[462]

In the same category are dreams which are the fruit of one's daytime reflections, the image of matters which one thought about or with which one was occupied. Regarding these the Talmud says: "The Roman emperor[463] said to R. Joshua [b. Hananya]: 'You Jews say you are very wise; tell me what I will see in my dream.' 'You will see the Persians making you do forced labor, robbing you, and making you feed unclean animals with a golden staff.' He thought about this all day, and at night he saw it in a dream." And so too [the Talmud recounts the following incident wherein] King Shapur of Persia said to Samuel, "You say you are very wise; tell me what I will see in my dream." "You will see the Romans come and capture you, forcing you to grind date-pits in a golden mill." He thought about this all day and in the night saw it in a dream.[464]

Dreams of these types are caused by a defect in the imaginative faculty, which forms and combines images, all of which are false—"they speak lies."[465] This occurs during sleep, when gases rise from the stomach to the brain, and the imaginative faculty mixes and confuses things.

The second major type of dream is the providential one, wherein Divine Providence is the Cause and the Informer. Dreams of this category are true and are revealed to morally perfect individuals, as in the case of the dreams of Joseph, though occasionally also to the wicked or to idol worshipers. This type of dream is of no aid or use to the dreamer, but is for the use of others. Thus, God revealed Himself to Avimelekh in honor of Abraham and of Isaac, his only son.[466] He also revealed Himself to Laban, to save Jacob, His chosen one.[467] The same kind of dream was revealed to Pharaoh's Butler and Baker, in order to raise and exalt Joseph, His righteous one.[468] And to Nebuchadnezzar, to console His people.[469] Of this type of dream our Rabbis, may their names be blessed, said, "A person is shown only the imaginings of his heart, as it is said, 'As for you, O king, your thoughts came into your mind on your bed,'[470] or if you wish, I may prove this from the following verse,[471] 'that you may know the thoughts of your heart.'"[472] This is because when the Holy One reveals Himself to someone who is not a prophet, He shows him things which he wants to know and has thought about during the day, as in the case of Nebuchadnezzar, in order to quiet his foreboding. And when he reveals Himself to men of spiritual and moral stature, He does so in order to inform them of good tidings or to tell them of their evil deeds in order that they repent and beg compassion in their anguish.

Further, regarding Rava's statement that "this is proved by the fact that one never dreams about a golden date palm or an elephant going through the eye of a needle,"[473] it seems that he brought proof from palpable matters, for generally people have dreams related to whatever they thought about during the day, and similarly, authentic dreams are made up of things the dreamer is concerned with, and which God, may He be blessed, reveals to him out of His love for him, as is said in Job 33[:15–16], "In a dream, in a night vision, when deep sleep falls on men, while they slumber in their beds. Then He opens men's understanding and signifies His discipline." In other words, then He reveals the decree which He has written and sealed as punishment in order to save them by means of repentance. And for this reason our Rabbis, blessed be their memory, said that a righteous person only has bad dreams, for a bad dream's sadness is sufficient for it,[474] and sadness is one aspect of repentance. So too they said, "Fasting is good for a dream, like fire for flax."[475] And since there is no completely righteous man on earth who does not sin,[476] dreams show the righteous person the evil intended for him, with the sound of terror in his ears— why do you slumber? rise, call out to your Lord![477]

These things are true and well established; their frequent occurrence proves their truth. Even though our Sages, blessed be their memory, said that "there is no dream without vain things interspersed,"[478] R. Simon bar Yohai has already taught us in Parashat Mikketz:[479] "To a righteous person nothing at all misleading is revealed." And in *Sefer Hasidim* you will see many such incidents.

These matters regarding providential dreams need no further proof, given their origin in Divine Providence, even though they do not come to a prophet. For after we were exiled from our land, and distanced from our soil, prophecy has ceased, the Urim and Tumim have been hidden away, and all that remains to us is the grace of dreams by which the Holy One, blessed be He, informs us of hidden things, as our Rabbis said in the first chapter of Hagigah: "Said Rava: 'Even though I will hide My Face from them on that day,' said the Holy One, blessed be He, 'in a dream will I speak to him.'"[480] Similarly, it is said that a dream is a sixtieth part of prophecy.[481] Furthermore, the leavings of prophecy are—dreams.[482]

The third category is the prophetic dream, namely, the dreams received by prophets who truly prophesy in God's name, and by dreams of this kind He reveals His secrets to His servants the prophets, as in the dreams of Jacob, Solomon, and Daniel.

And if you wish to know the difference between authentic prophetic dreams and natural dreams, it is that the authentic prophetic dream produces a tremendous impression on several levels. The effect on the prophet's soul is so great that he recognizes immediately that he has been granted Divine grace. As the Rambam wrote in the *Guide of the Perplexed*, I:45: "the prophecy announces itself to the prophet"; and so too did Jeremiah give witness: "A burning fire was in my heart."[483] The effect in the soul of the dreamer who has an authentic dream is on a lower level. However, even confused dreams, arising from the imaginative faculty, have some effect.[484] And so our Sages, blessed be their memory, laid down the rule that one who dreams, and is sad upon awakening, should go and sweeten it.[485] And so too Job 4[:13–14]: "In thought-filled visions of the night, when deep sleep falls on men, fear and trembling came upon me, making all my bones quake with fear." This occurs with all authentic dreams that are accompanied by trembling, as you find with the dreams of Pharaoh and Nebuchadnezzar.

Thus, to sum up, there are three categories of dreams; some of them are authentic, and some confused.

Therefore, the Sages said in tractate Berakhot: "Rabbah contrasted two verses: 'In a dream I speak to him,'[486] and 'the dreams speak falsely.'[487] There is no contradiction; the first refers to dreams mediated by an angel, the second to those mediated by a demon."[488] The commentators explain that authentic dreams come by means of an angel, and natural ones by means of the imaginative faculty, which is called a "demon." But they are wrong, for dreams which come through a demon are just that: demonic dreams. This opinion is held by many writers perfect in their knowledge, who prepared themselves to accept demonic influences in a dream. And so too the Rambam, in speaking of the prohibition of eating blood, wrote in his *Guide,* III:46: "They imagined that with this deed the demons ate the blood which is their food, and they eat the meat. In this way there is love between them, and the demons come to them in a dream, or so they think, and tell them of future occurrences, etc."

This explanation is indubitably correct. For if you do not accept it, what does this verse come to tell us? Do we not know that dreams are imaginary—they speak vainly? Quite definitely the verse refers to dreams which truly come by means of demons.

Appendix Two

In which is explained the matter of dreams and the difference between a dream that comes by means of an angel and one that comes by means of a demon— written by the great scholar, R. Judah Moses Ftayya (author of *Bet Lehem Yehudah*), in his work *Minhat Yehudah Haruhot Mesapperot,* p. 31, Parashat Mikketz.

"In the morning his Pharaoh's heart pounded."[489] It seems from this that his mind was not disturbed while he was asleep and dreaming, but in the morning when he awoke and pondered his dream. The same phrase is found in regard to Nebuchadnezzar's dream—"his spirit was troubled and sleep was taken from him."[490] The dream awakened him, and, troubled, he could not go back to sleep. That is the way of a true angelic dream: the dreamer is troubled only after awakening, but not while dreaming. The dream has this effect because the Creator does not wish to frighten the dreamer but only to inform him of what has been decreed concerning him or others, in order that they will attend to repenting for their sins. Thus there is no need to frighten them in their sleep.

The same holds for Isaiah's prophecy regarding King Hezekiah, whom he informed that he would "die and not live"[491]—as our Sages interpreted this, he would die in this world and have no portion in the world to come. When Hezekiah asked Isaiah the reason for this harsh decree, he was told that it was because he had not occupied himself with the commandment of having children. "If so," said the king, "give me your daughter to wife." "The decree has already been enacted." Hezekiah then answered, "Ben Amotz,[492] stop prophesying and leave! I have a tradition from my father's father's house—from King David, may he rest in peace—that a person should not deprive himself of Divine mercy even when a sharp sword rests on his neck! For if the decree has indeed been issued and there is no hope, why did God send you to me? Don't you have any good tidings to give me?"[493]

This applies to any evil dream which comes to a person through the medium of an angel. If the decree cannot be reversed by means of prayer, fasting, charity, and repentance, why does he have the dream? As our Sages

131

commented on the verse "the Lord has so made it that they [i.e., God's creations] should fear Him,"[494] this refers to an evil dream, and only in order that He should be feared. Thus there is no reason for the dreamer to be troubled during the dream.

The essential characteristic of an angelic dream is that it is orderly, with no extraneous material mixed in. Furthermore, the dreamer should not be panicked or frightened at the time of dreaming; and he must see himself as though truly awake in the dream. If all these conditions are fulfilled, you may be certain that the dream is true, and that it comes through an angel and is a one-sixtieth part of prophecy.[495]

However, a dream which comes by means of a demon is quite different. The demon stands near the person as he dozes and whispers frightening words, a concoction of many things, into his ears. This arouses frightening images in the dozer's mind; his heart beats wildly and he awakes in a panic.[496] The demons remain at his side, rejoicing and toying with his mind in order to frighten him; when he falls sleep they begin again. After this happens several times,[497] he finally begins preparing for bed by reciting the Keri'at Shema prayer, or deals with them some other way. He awakens and recites "Unclean, unclean! Flee from here!" three times. At that the demon will go on his way, and the sleeper will be able to rest, secure from such dreams. If he has an enemy [who may have sent the demons to him] he recites the following: "Unclean, unclean! Flee from here and go to so-and-so and frighten him!" And then the demon will do everything he commands.

If you want to try out this remedy, whisper into the ear of a sleeping child, "I have bought you apples and nuts; they are in a box near you." When the child awakens, he will ask where the apples and nuts are, as is written in *Sefer Hasidim,* chapter 441 (see below).

In sum, frightening evil dreams mostly come while a person dozes, either at the beginning or the end of his sleep, when he is beginning to awaken and his mind is able to perceive images, and not when he is sleeping deeply.

If someone recites the Keri'at Shema before going to sleep, but afterward is aroused by the sound of a sleeping child, in order to cover it or for some similar reason, the demons have the power to frighten him with evil visions when he returns to bed. To prevent this, he should recite Keri'at Shema, or at least the first verse and the next—"Blessed, etc."—as is explained in the Gate of Verses, in the section on Song of Songs, on the verse "I am asleep."[498]

Furthermore, if a man or a woman is possessed by a succubus or an incubus that seeks to have intercourse with him or her, it may overcome the protection afforded by the Keri'at Shema in order to satisfy its lust. In that case, a simple

Keri'at Shema will not suffice; instead, concentration on every word is necessary, and even this may not protect the one who recites it.

I also have new information to impart. Demons understand what kinds of
things bother people when they see them in a dream, such as dreaming that
one's teeth are falling out, or that an atoning chicken is being whirled around
one's head,[499] or that an animal is being slaughtered in front of oneself, or
[perhaps] seeing oneself fasting or dressed in black, or walking barefoot,[500] or
something similar. Do not worry about such dreams unless you see yourself
being sworn in the dream, or are called by name to go up to the reading of the
Torah. In any case, if you do not worry even in these cases, may you be
blessed.[501]

Likewise, demons sometimes show a person evil things, and if the dreamer
is a fool who believes in the dream, they attempt to accomplish the evil thing
in reality in order to deceive him [further] into believing in his dreams. Or, at
least, when they hear the decree in Heaven regarding some evil which ought
never come to pass,[502] they then inform the person so that he believes in these
dreams. The dreamer must know, however, that if he fasts in order to mitigate
the force of the dream, or performs some atoning action, or redeems his soul
[by means of charity], but does not inquire of a wise person who knows how
to distinguish between demonic [and angelic] dreams, he is destined to have
equally harsh, evil dreams in the future, for demons rejoice in not having
labored in vain in deceiving this person. Demons of this kind are called "foreign
demons, expert in doing harm."

There are other demons, so-called "Jewish demons," who have different
habits. Some disguise themselves to look like the early prophets or the Tannaim,
and others assume the appearance of the judges of Israel or of famous scholars
who have departed this world, with great beards and a crown on their heads,[503]
or as the righteous and pious ones; occasionally, they appear even as the
Patriarchs Abraham, Isaac, and Jacob, or Elijah the Prophet, or similar figures.
The person to whom they show themselves must ask them whether they are
indeed the Fathers of the World[504] or perhaps merely have similar names—so
too should he ask Elijah. He must carefully examine the answer, for if they
respond unclearly and ambiguously, he can be certain that they are demons.

These demons can do even greater things—they can show him a semblance
of the Firmament, a semblance of the Heavenly Throne, the heavenly host, and
similar matters. They take care not to frighten the dreamer.[505] On the contrary,
they tell him to earnestly study such and such an amount of Zohar and Psalms,
and to rise at night to recite Tikkun Hatzot.[506] Sometimes they decree that he
should immerse himself in a mikveh[507] several times a day, change his clothing,

and take care not to touch his wife.[508] After that they add ascetic practices and
fasts; if he does not perform these, they beat him and emphatically warn him
not to reveal these visions to anyone else (so that no one will recognize that they
are the result of demonic dreams). This continues until by and by he is drawn
after them and his thoughts are tied to them. Gradually he goes insane and in
the end comes down with epilepsy, God forbid. At first these demons come in
a dream at the beginning of sleep, but afterwards they come even when he is
awake. Sometimes they come at first during a waking period. Several people
have brought me children who see visions while awake; space does not allow
me to give all the details, but I will recount one case as an example.

In the year 5671 [1911], in the month of Tammuz, after the Sabbath
Afternoon Prayer, they brought me an eleven-year-old boy who claimed he
could speak directly to the prophet Elijah, who would show him visions
(hiddot). Whenever he wished to speak with him he could call him and instantly
Elijah would come; the only proviso was that they must be alone, away from
people, with no one else present. I said to him, "Come into this room and ask
him if he is truly Elijah the Prophet." He did so, and answered, "Yes, I am
Elijah; why does Judah" (he called me by name) "doubt my identity?" "That
isn't Elijah," I said to the boy, "but a Jewish demon whose name happens to
be Elijah, but he is not Elijah the Prophet. You have been harmed by one of
the Jewish demons; come and I will recite the Prayer for the Harmed over you,
and this Elijah-demon will leave you." The child insisted that it was Elijah the
Prophet. "Do whatever you want and we will see whose word comes true."
After I recited the prayer over him two or three times, the lad went into the
other room to see if Elijah would come. And behold, Elijah immediately came,
as was his wont. I was amazed at this, and took the boy to the Hakham R.
Simon Aaron Agasi, may his memory be for a blessing, who was still alive at
that time. After testing him, he decided that it was indeed Elijah the Prophet,
and not a demon. I disagreed with him and insisted that it was a demon. We
then agreed that after the Sabbath ended we would all go to the Hakham R.
Jacob, son of the Hakham R. Joseph Hayyim, in order to test him. After the
latter had tested him in several ways, he too decided that this was without doubt
Elijah the Prophet, may his memory be for a blessing. I disagreed with the two
of them, and refuted their arguments. I asked permission from them to test him
further. Then I told the boy to go and tell Elijah to translate the verse in
Jeremiah, chapter 10[:11]: "So shall you say to them: may the gods, which did
not make the heavens and the earth, perish from the earth and from beneath
these heavens." If he translated this verse into Arabic, then it would be possible
to consider whether he was indeed Elijah the Prophet and not a demon. This

is because even though demons understand Aramaic[509]—after all, they show evil dreams to those who speak Aramaic, and whisper in their ears—they do not wish to hear this verse recited or translate it, since it speaks in their disfavor. When the boy asked Elijah to translate the verse, Elijah replied, "I cannot linger here; I must go in order to record the merits of Israel." When the lad gave me this answer, I said to him, "Go to him again and tell him to translate the verse! [Tell him] 'It is necessary for you to do this to substantiate your claim that you are indeed Elijah.'" Once again Elijah responded, "I have already told you that I must go." "Say to Elijah," I ordered him, "'It would have been easier for him to translate the verse while we were standing here rather than to debate whether you should. The scholars here will not be satisfied until you do so!'" When the boy repeated these words to Elijah, he grew angry and swore, "As the Name[510] lives! I will no longer appear to you because you do not believe that I am Elijah." He immediately departed, and never again appeared to the boy.

After Elijah left, the aforementioned scholars told me that it seemed to them that this really had been Elijah the Prophet, for he customarily swore using the expression "As God lives."[511] Our Rabbis, may their memory be blessed, have already commented that we have a tradition that demons do not use the Name of Heaven in vain.[512]

I continued to insist that he had been a demon, and that he had not uttered the Name of Heaven in vain, because he had sworn not to return and had fulfilled his oath, since he had not returned. Moreover, the Name of Heaven was not involved in any case, since he had not uttered the Tetragrammaton, or even the Name as it is customarily pronounced (Adonai). Rather, he had used the letters heh, shin, mem, which spell the word Hashem, "the Name." His oath was thus only a means of misleading us. On hearing this the scholars agreed with my analysis of the situation.

Let us return to our original subject. To this point we have discussed the difference between angelic dreams and dreams which come by means of "foreign demons" or "Jewish demons." We will now return to the subject of the character of dreams themselves and their decipherment; this I will begin, with God's help.

Know that dreams come symbolically[513] for several reasons. One is that they may [be intended as predictions] for as many as several years in the future. Second, a dream may come to reprove the dreamer for some sin he has committed. Third, it may relate to matters which concern relations between him and his wife. I will cite an example of each type.

The first category may be illustrated by Joseph's dream about his brothers[514] or Nebuchadnezzar's dream about the idol[515]—all of these are presented symbolically because they are intended for the future; the more allusive the dream, the further off its fulfillment.

The second category are dreams which come to reprove the dreamer for some sin. [For example,] a man once came and told me about a dream in which he tied his head tefillin onto his arm and his arm tefillin onto his head. I explained to him that, because of his greatness of soul, this was meant as a reproof for having unnatural intercourse with his wife, so that he would refrain from such practices in the future.

On another occasion a man came and told me that he had had the same dream three times. "I saw worms issuing from my left thigh; I do not know the meaning of this dream." I told him that he had slept with a Muslim woman three times, and that was why he had three times been shown worms in his thigh, since the sin began there, as it is written [regarding a woman suspected of adultery]: "[the bitter waters will make . . .] the thigh to sag."[516] Gentiles [I continued] are of the left side[517] of Israel, for Isaac and Ishmael[518] were brothers. The man admitted his sin and repented.

Another time there was a woman who chattered to everyone, Jew and Gentile alike, and conducted herself brazenly. Her husband was told in a dream that she was the wife of a high priest. I told him that this meant that he should not involve himself in her burial (that is, she had played the harlot).[519] However, I did not hear afterwards whether this was true or not.

The third category involves matters relating to relations between man and wife. For example, once there was a rabbinical student who studied every weeknight in various yeshivot, once in this one and once in another, following the schedule of each and not spending the night at home except for Friday nights. Since he had remained awake most of the week, a deep sleep descended on him on Friday evenings. One Friday night he dreamed that a man said to him, "A righteous person comes to his table," but he did not understand what this meant. The man came to him again and said, "All good to the discerning man." He suddenly realized that this referred to his marital obligations to his wife.[520]

Once it happened that a scholar had a dream on a Friday night. It seemed to be Shavuot night, and he was studying with his family.[521] He brought nine wicks and placed them in three earthenware vessels, three in each lamp. He put sesame oil into the vessels and lit them, though he was surprised to find himself lighting earthenware vessels, which do not transmit light well as glass lanterns. Observing the vessels, he noted that whenever the wicks were high above the rims of the vessels, the light would spill out in all directions, reaching the walls of the house, but when the tops of the wicks were burnt down, and the flame was below the rims of the vessels, near the oil reservoirs, the light would be directed only upward toward the heavens—and then he awoke from his dream.

Since the scholar had once had four sons, one of whom had died, leaving only three, he was deeply affected and concerned by this dream. He was worried about his three surviving sons, and decided to fast even though it was the Sabbath.[522] After the eighth hour of the day, he unexpectedly met me on the street. He told me his dream, and informed me that he was fasting. I gave his dream a simple interpretation which did not satisfy him. He begged me to give him the true interpretation.

"If I interpret the dream for you in a true fashion," I said to him, "you must not contradict me and reject the interpretation. [First] you must give me your word that you will acknowledge the truth, and then I will interpret it. He agreed to my terms, and I told him that on Friday night, "You were sleeping in your bed alone and your wife was likewise in hers. Three times you awoke to fulfill your marital obligation, feeling desire for your wife, but each time in the end you refrained and did not fulfill your marital obligation. That is why you had this dream."

"Believe me," he responded, "that is exactly how it happened, no more and no less! But tell me, how did you know?" I explained, "The three wicks of the lamp were the three flames of love[523] that issue from the two thighs[524] of a righteous person. You lit them three times, but the flames were subdued within the earthenware vessel, not shedding their light properly. You ought to be aware of the principle that most angelic dreams can be explained in Kabbalistic terms, since the angel is a spiritual being, and their symbols will tend in this direction. Moreover, especially in matters like this, which involve marital affairs, the symbols will be very indirect. You were shown this dream because they were being strict with you for neglecting your marital duties." And he answered, "You have consoled me; may God bless you."

Since we have come to the subject of dreams and their interpretation, I will record a few dreams whose interpretations I was asked to provide; possibly those who study my book will learn to interpret dreams in the same way. I once visited an ophthalmologist, Ezekiel Ezra ben Moshe Al 'Eini by name. Aside from eye diseases, he also knew how to compound a certain ointment which cured that bone disease which causes pain within the flesh, something not known to all physicians in his generation. [Naturally,] this ointment was very expensive. When I came in, he told me that he had seen his father, Moses, who had been dead for thirty years, that very night—the first time he had ever appeared to him in a dream. His father had asked him, "I beg of you, my son, accompany me just to the city of Basra; do me this favor and I will not ask any other"—so was the dream.

The physician was very depressed and wished to know the meaning of his dream. Before I explain the dream I must inform the reader of this man's behavior and habits, since I knew him well. The man Moses was exceedingly humble,[525] an elder of dignified appearance, and one who was involved in the pursuit of doing mitzvot. He customarily attended three synagogues that were adjacent to each other in one place. He would enter one in order to answer amen to the Kaddish, Barekhu, and Kedusha prayers. He would always go from one to the other. And when he saw a scholar[526] who had come from afar, he would quickly sit down in order to rise before him when he approached. After prayers he would gather all the merchants in the synagogue in order to put on garments with tzitzit [ritual fringes][527] and tefillin, and to read the Shema. He would buy fringed garments and tefillin for them out of his own money and donate them [to the synagogue] so that they would always be available. This was his custom day by day.

Now we will interpret the dream which the son, the aforementioned physician, dreamed. I told the physician that his father had been transmigrated into a certain man who was missing [i.e., had failed to perform] a particular mitzvah. The man in question had an illness of the eyes or the bones, but was poor and could not afford to pay a physician to treat him. "He will come to you today or tomorrow; your father has come to ask you not to be harsh with him, but to treat him for free, for he is really your father. This affair will last only three or four days, as long as it takes to get to Basra; after that the man will leave. [How will you recognize him?] Presumably he will be in the habit of providing fringed garments and tefillin for others. When this occurs, please send for me so that we may both see the wonders of the God of Knowledge."

I had hardly reached my house when the physician's messenger came and told me that the man of whom I had spoken had come, and was afflicted with a disease of the legs. When I arrived at the physician's house, I saw that the man was very poor. He was in the sesame oil trade and had formerly employed several workers, but now, because of his many sins, strangers had consumed the fruits of his work[528] and he was left with nothing. Not only that, but he had an illness which affected his legs and he could not walk because of the pain.

"Perhaps," I said to him, "perhaps this was because you did not wear ritual fringes or tefillin?" "Not only was I careful in regard to prayer, tzitzit, and tefillin," he answered, "but I used to buy tefillin for my workers and not let them begin work until they had put them on. And at mealtimes I would instruct them to recite the grace after meals, even though this caused me a loss. I do not know why God has treated me so."

The physician then followed his father's instructions and told the patient, "Don't be afraid; I will treat you as well as I can." He also gave him money to support his household, and after three days he left.

[After this visit] the physician was greatly distressed, saying that if his father, a pious man who customarily accomplished great things, was treated this way [because of some minor failing, how much more severely would he himself be treated]! "How can I confess my sins and justify my iniquities!" He fasted for several days, confessed his sins before God, and became completely righteous, remaining so until his death.

Another time there was a pious man who fasted every day of the week except for the Sabbath; but when he ate the Sabbath meals he suffered abdominal pain because his body was not used to eating regular meals. He decided to fast on the Sabbath as well if the Rabbis, may God preserve them, allowed him to. Before he had a chance to ask their permission to fast on the Sabbath, however, he saw the following in a dream: Two men offered him two plates, one filled with fruit and the other with vegetables, telling him to eat. He did not want to eat, for it seemed to him that he was fasting, as was his custom. The men begged him to the point of embarrassment, but he refused to give in to them. At that point they became angry, and one said to the other, "Let's go; take the plates away from him, for he clearly has no interest in the Resurrection of the Dead!"—such was his dream.

When he awoke from his sleep he was trembling from fear of having lost his right to be resurrected, and he sent a messenger to me to ask for an interpretation; he did not come himself because he did not want to be identified as the person who had fasted all week.

I explained to the messenger that there are souls which have been trans-migrated into water, salt and bread, fruit, meat, fish, and fowl. By means of the blessings a person recites over these foods, the souls within them are renewed and go on to complete their sentences in Gehenna.[529] If blessings are not recited over the foods, and they are eaten without a blessing, the souls are in great pain because they have not merited being renewed. As a result, anyone who eats them without having recited a blessing is condemned to be transmigrated into the same foods when he dies. The Creator arranges matters so that these foods come to a person who will eat them without reciting a blessing so that they will not merit renewal; they are requited measure for measure for not having recited the proper blessings in their turn.

This is the secret of the verse "for man does not live by bread alone, [but only on the word of God]."[530] In other words, a man transmigrated into bread does not live by bread without a blessing, but only on the utterance of God's Mouth—the blessing recited over it. It is by this that a man transmigrated into bread lives. Now the man who dreamed this dream, who fasted every weekday without the excuse of atoning for some sin he had committed, caused many holy sparks[531] and many transmigrated souls to remain imprisoned in the food over which he did not recite a blessing because he was fasting. For this reason Heaven told him that he need not fast any more, and from now on must eat in order to revive the transmigrated dead with that food. And because he did not wish to eat, they said that he was not interested in the Resurrection of the Dead . . . but not that he himself would not rise from the dead.

It seems to me that this is the intent of the verse "He loved cursing, and it came to him; he did not wish blessing, and it remained far from him."[532] The verse refers to a wicked person who eats without reciting a blessing; such a person harms both himself and the souls in the food; this is the meaning of "he did not wish blessing." What does the Holy One, blessed be He, do? He provides food for him which does not contain transmigrated souls, for these souls are transmigrated and cry out to the Holy One, blessed be He, that he not give them over to the consumption of that person lest he ruin them still more; this is the meaning of "he did not wish blessing, and it remained far from him."

On another occasion there was a plague in our city, God forbid; a man known as Ezekiel the Persian, who studied in our yeshiva and had a mother and father, brother and sister, was there. His mother was stricken with the plague one night and died the next morning. Because of the plague the seven days of mourning were not observed. The next night the scholar dreamed that his father's right eye had been plucked out. He came to me that day, trembling and frightened lest he die as well because he was the eldest son and a scholar besides; there was no doubt that he was his father's "right eye." I told him that the interpretation of the dream was that it referred to his father's head tefillin, which had an invalid letter in it. "[Moreover," I said,] "I can tell you that the problem letter is in the second parchment,[533] that is, Exodus 13:5, for according to the secret of the matter, that dream refers to the five kindnesses of Daat, which are five times the gematria[534] of the Tetragrammaton,[535] yielding 130, which is equivalent to the word ayin, 'eye.'[536] I can also say that the problem letter is in the first line, for there the word ve-la-avotekha, 'and to your fathers' is written."

The young scholar objected that his father's tefillin had been examined just a month before, but I replied that there must be an invalid letter. He immediately went and got his father's head-tefillin; I undid the threads and pulled the second parchment from its place. Having done this, I showed the yeshiva students how the final kaf of the word ve-la-avotekha had its "roof" torn so that it was divided into two letters, a final nun and a dot next to it. The student was relieved that the invalidity refered to his father's tefillin and not to himself. This interpretation was a wonderment in the eyes of the entire study hall.

On yet another occasion a pregnant woman came to me. In a dream she had seen her husband go to the cemetery. He drew his dead brother's body from there and brought it home, whereupon she argued with her husband that he must take the corpse out of the house. The husband paid no attention, took the body up to the roof, and buried it there.[537]

I asked her how many steps there were from the courtyard to the roof; she replied that she did not know the exact number. I told her that there were nine steps. "Sir," she said to me, "I think there are more, perhaps as many as twelve." "In that case," I replied, "I will not interpret your dream until you have gone home, counted the steps, and returned. She did so, and on her return laughingly said that there were indeed nine steps, as I had said.

I then told her, "This is the interpretation. You are pregnant with a son who is the transmigrated soul of your dead brother-in-law, the child's uncle. When he is born you must name him after his uncle; you are being informed by this angelic dream that you will carry a full nine months, corresponding to the aforementioned nine steps; you will not have a miscarriage. After that the boy will live, and not die as his uncle did, but he will remain "buried" with you in the house and not return to the cemetery."

And so it was. She carried her baby to term, then had a son and named him after his uncle; afterwards she came to the study hall and thanked me gratefully.

Finally, an old woman once came and told me that she had dreamed that she had taken a Torah scroll out of the ark in order to read from it during public prayers; another woman came and snatched it away from her. I said: "This is the interpretation. You will be given a child to present for circumcision at the throne of Elijah."[538] Another woman, I continued, would come and snatch the child from her and she would merit bringing the child to Elijah's throne. The woman replied that this very thing had happened to her two weeks before (as if to say, "Are we shown past events in dreams?")—and asked me, "Then is this the correct interpretation?"

I asked her when she had actually had the dream, and she replied that it had been about a month before. "If so," I said, "the dream occurred before the incident, and so it was by no means a case of your being shown a past event in a dream. But what can I do if you come to ask for an interpretation only after it has come to pass!"

Know that a Torah scroll generally represents a son. And therefore if a person buys a Torah scroll or is given a scroll in a dream, it means that his wife will become pregnant with a son.

If a Torah scroll falls from his hand in a dream, his wife will miscarry. If it is torn, the child will die. This is a tried and proven interpretation.

Finally, some dreams are confused and disorganized, but do not let them worry or frighten you. Dreams of this kind come from the imagination, for the mind is not quietly at rest during sleep. They are of no account, either for good or for evil, and there is no need to be concerned about them.

These then are some of the methods of dream interpretation; let the wise listen and increase their knowledge.[539]

Notes

1 Shortened from a semi-poetic introductory paragraph.

2 Amos 3:7.

3 See Talmud Bava Batra 12b.

4 Zohar I:183b, with minor differences from the standard edition.

5 Or: "the plethora" (*shefa*).

6 Deuteronomy 31:18.

7 Following Numbers 12:6.

8 Hagigah 5b.

9 I cannot identify this writer; the name is not mentioned by G. E. von Grunebaum in the article on Islamic dream interpretation in the volume edited by him and Roger Caillois, *The Dream and Human Societies* (Berkeley and Los Angeles: University of California Press, 1966).

10 Job 33:14–16.

11 NJPS: "pride." The word *gevah* may be also be interpreted as "a body," and hence, the essence of the matter, as the author proceeds to explain. The verse thus refers to the essence which is hidden from men; as a result, people no longer attempt to interpret dreams.

12 Job 33:17.

13 See Jeremiah 3:14.

14 Berakhot, chap. 9.

15 Despite the author's assertion above that such people were rarely to be found.

16 See Berakhot 55b; in our editions this statement is attributed to R. Bizna b. Zabda in the name of R. Akiva in the name of R. Panda, who had it from R. Nahum in the name of R. Biryam through a certain elder who is identified as R. Bana'ah; in some manuscripts, however, the elder is identified as R. Nehorai. As we shall see, Almoli often quotes the Florence manuscript.

17 Genesis 40:8. The usual rendering of *Elokim* is "God," but it is occasionally rendered "judges" or "master," as in Exodus 4:16 and 21:6.

18 Psalms 92:6.

19 Following I Samuel 3:1.

20 Isaiah 29:9.

21 Isaiah 29:7–8.

22 Isaiah 29:9.

23 Ibid. NJPS translates: "Act blind and be blinded!" but R. Almoli relates the words *hishta'ashe'u va-sho'u* to the Aramaic *she'i*, "to speak."

24 This point is frequently made by Ibn Ezra and others; see, for example, Ibn Ezra on Jonah 2:2.

25 Ibid.

26 Isaiah 29:10.

27 Paraphrasing the verse just cited.

28 Isaiah 29:11.

29 Malachi 3:16.

30 Berakhot 14a.

31 Isaiah 29:13.

32 Ibid.

33 Isaiah 29:14.

34 Ibid.

35 Genesis 41:39.

36 Psalms 82:5.

37 The Rishonim.

38 A dream interpreter who lived in the time of Rava and Abaye, the two great fourth-century Amoraim; see chap. 2 below.

39 Berakhot 56a.

40 Alluding to Numbers 7:14.

41 Psalms 102:14.

42 These sections have not been included in the translation.

43 Genesis 28:12–16.

44 Daniel 10–12.

45 I Kings 3:4–15.

46 Berakhot 57b.

47 I.e., dreams that come to those who are not prophets or those who are divinely inspired.

48 Genesis 37:5–10.

49 Genesis 41:1–7.

50 Genesis 40:9–12.

51 Genesis 40:16–17.

52 Genesis 20:3.

53 Genesis 31:24.

54 Genesis 20:11.

55 *Guide of the Perplexed* II:41.

56 As is his custom, R. Almoli goes into great and to some extent repetitive

detail on each point; in these instances the translation has been shortened, as indicated.

57 Deuteronomy 13:2.

58 Jeremiah 23:25, 27.

59 One of Job's "comforters."

60 Job 33:14–17. Literally, the first verse means: "For God speaks in once, or twice."

61 Genesis 46:2.

62 Of spirits and the like.

63 The Hebrew word *mosar*, usually related to *yaser* and translated as "disciplining" is here understood as related to *hesir*, to remove.

64 Shabbat 92b.

65 Guide II:44.

66 Genesis 28:12–13. R. Almoli proceeds with further proofs for this contention, drawn from the dreams of Solomon and Daniel referred to above.

67 Numbers 12:6; the Talmudic passage is from Hagigah 5a.

68 Deuteronomy 5:4. R. Almoli proceeds to give additional examples of the use of this phrase.

69 R. Almoli continues with numerous other proofs for this contention.

70 Abraham ben Samuel Ibn Hasdai, early 13th cent.

71 *Ben Ha-Melekh veha-Nazir;* an edition of this work was printed at Constantinople in 1518, three years after R. Almoli's own work, but Ibn Hasdai was presumably available to him in manuscript.

72 A number of proofs for this contention follow.

73 Genesis 28:12–16.

74 I Kings 3:4–15.

75 Kohelet 5:2.

76 Daniel 7:1.

77 Lit., "written."

78 Zohar I:199b–200a.

79 I.e., from the realm of Good.

80 The side of evil, of demons.

81 Jeremiah 23:32.

82 Jeremiah 23:37.

83 Numbers 12:6.

84 Ibid.

85 Ibid.

86 Zohar I:193a.

87 Numbers 12:13.

[88] Zechariah 10:2.

[89] Berakhot 55b.

[90] Lit., "do not cause to ascend or descend," i.e., have no effect.

[91] Genesis Rabba 68:12.

[92] Jeremiah 29:8.

[93] R. Almoli proceeds to derive a proof for this contention from Job 33:14-17.

[94] Numbers 12:6.

[95] See Genesis 37:9.

[96] See Genesis 37:5–7.

[97] Genesis 41:28.

[98] See Rashi on Genesis 47:19.

[99] Genesis 41:13.

[100] Berakhot, chap. 9.

[101] Berakhot 57b.

[102] Lit., "unripe fruit." Just as sleep is a shadow of death, and the Sabbath a shadow of the delights of the World to Come; see Genesis Rabba 17:5.

[103] Taanit 9a–9b.

[104] Corrected from "Rav and Samuel b . . ."

[105] In current editions: Idi.

[106] In current editions: "wink."

[107] Zechariah 11:8.

[108] In current editions "go in peace," which implies that they were about to die; R. Almoli's version is similar to that of MSS Munich 95 and 140, which read "to peace," the greeting given to the living. In either case, this shows the seriousness with which R. Papa took the dream.

[109] Berakhot 55b.

[110] Zechariah 10:2.

[111] Kohelet 5:2.

[112] Since the Talmud states that "a dream which is not interpreted is like a letter which is not read" (Berakhot 55a) one would assume that interpreting a dream would ensure its fulfillment.

[113] Zechariah 10:2.

[114] Numbers 12:6; see Berakhot 55b.

[115] This section is not translated in this edition. The question of why dreams occur while the dreamer is asleep is touched on again in the next gate.

[116] R. Levi b. Gershon (1288–1344), famous philosopher and biblical exegete, mathematician and astronomer. Aside from his biblical commentaries, his best-known work is his *Wars of the Lord,* in which he presents his philosophy.

[117] Perhaps a reference to Solomon b. Moses of Melgueuil's thirteenth-century translation from the Latin, called *Ha-Sheinah veha-Yekitzah*, to which I have no access. Alternatively, it may be a reference to Avicenna's *Canon*, which was available in Hebrew.

[118] Kohelet 5:2.

[119] I.e., the "other," left side, the side of evil.

[120] Zohar I:199b. R. Almoli's text differs slightly from the printed version; the translation reflects his text.

[121] *Istiqdon*, presumably a by-form of *istikton;* see Samuel Krauss, *Griechische und Lateinische Lehnwoerter im Talmud, Midrasch und Targum*, II, p. 80a.

[122] *Miriyon.*

[123] *Shiqmonia*, presumably some product of the sycamore; see Immanuel Loew, *Die Flora der Juden*, I, p. 275. Sycamore resin was used medicinally.

[124] See Immanuel Loew, *Die Flora der Juden* I, pp. 526–527.

[125] *Mayorana;* see Immanuel Loew, *Die Flora der Juden* II, pp. 73–74.

[126] I cannot identify this food substance.

[127] In Leviticus 11:43 it is written without an *alef.*

[128] Yoma 39a.

[129] Berakhot 55b, usually understood to mean that dreams follow their interpretation, i.e., that things foretold in a dream come to pass in real life more or less in accordance with the way the dream is interpreted.

[130] I.e., the angel in charge of dreams.

[131] Berakhot 57a; actually, the dream discussed there concerns adultery with a married woman. R. Almoli refers to this Talmudic passage more accurately in Part Two.

[132] In the text: "That one." Either R. Manasseh was quoting from memory or he had a different version than that in our editions of the Talmud.

[133] Both incidents are from Berakhot 56a.

[134] See Gate Four, Chapter Three below for a discussion of the Talmudic statement that "a person is only shown [in a dream] some of the thoughts of his heart" (Berakhot 55a), which seems to contradict this thesis.

[135] Psalms 91:10.

[136] In current editions: "R. Hisda said in the name of R. Jeremiah."

[137] Berakhot 55b.

[138] Kohelet 3:14.

[139] Berakhot 55a.

[140] Alluding to I Samuel 3:1.

[141] Genesis 41:11.

[142] Genesis 37:11.

[143] Genesis Rabba 84:12.

[144] Berakhot 55b.

[145] Job 32–33. Isaac Arundi was a fourteenth-century philosophical writer who lived in Italy and perhaps also Provence. Aside from his commentary on Job, he wrote a philosophical work called *Wars of the Lord,* directed against Gersonides' work of the same name. R. Almoli apparently saw the work in manuscript.

[146] Hullin 62a.

[147] Lit., "hint."

[148] See Gersonides' *Wars of the Lord,* bk. II, chap. 5; in Seymour Feldman's translation, vol. 2 (Philadelphia: Jewish Publication Society, 1987), p. 48.

[149] Referring to astrological conjunctions, etc.

[150] In Gates Seven and especially Eight below, R. Almoli discusses the effect that proper interpretation has on the fulfillment of prophetic dreams.

[151] Genesis 42:9.

[152] As in Berakhot 55a.

[153] Zohar I, 119b.

[154] See Gersonides' *Wars of the Lord,* bk. II, chap. 4; in Seymour Feldman's translation (see above, n. 148), vol. 2, pp. 42–47.

[155] 1126–1198, a Muslim commentator of Aristotle.

[156] Malachi 2:11.

[157] Deuteronomy 8:11.

[158] Which is taken in Jewish tradition as an exact description of the workings of Divine Providence.

[159] Berakhot 55b.

[160] Ibid. That is, he does not see things which he generally does not think about.

[161] Lit., "its interpretation."

[162] In the text: "That one." R. Manasseh was either quoting from memory or had a different version than that in our editions of the Talmud.

[163] Both incidents are from Berakhot 56a.

[164] R. Almoli presumably refers to the following argument from that chapter: "It is hardly likely that the meaning of these passages is that these dreams come true because the thought had been planted in these kings' minds; this is improbable. Moreover, if it were so, anyone could think 'good thoughts' during the day so as to have good dreams at night and assure a happy future for himself!"

[165] A Spanish Jewish philosopher who lived in the second half of the fifteenth century, and author of a classic commentary on Maimonides' *Guide of the Perplexed.*

[166] Genesis 28:12.

[167] Ibid.

[168] Genesis 37:7.

[169] Genesis 37:9.

[170] Genesis 41:1. For the passage, see Tanhuma Buber, Vayetze 6.

[171] Or: "style," Hebrew *signon*.

[172] Genesis 41:1.

[173] Genesis Rabba 89:4.

[174] Genesis 41:25.

[175] Zohar I, 194b.

[176] Lit., "eunuchs."

[177] Yoma 87b.

[178] Berakhot 55a.

[179] Genesis 41:13.

[180] Berakhot 55b.

[181] Since each of the interpretations given to R. Nehorai came to pass, the same should happen in this case as well.

[182] Genesis 41:39.

[183] Daniel 1:17.

[184] Alluding to Jeremiah 3:14.

[185] Genesis 41:16.

[186] Echoing Genesis 41:28.

[187] Genesis 41:8.

[188] See Genesis Rabba 89:6.

[189] In Gate Two.

[190] Rashi's successors as Talmud interpreters in the eleventh and twelfth centuries.

[191] Tosafot Berakhot 55a, s.v. *poterei*.

[192] I Samuel 3:1.

[193] Proverbs 10:4.

[194] Genesis 40:5.

[195] Genesis Rabba 68:12.

[196] Genesis Rabba 68:2.

[197] There is a slight confusion in the text, which has, literally, "follows the interpreter that the inquirer after the dream . . ."

[198] Exodus 4:11.

[199] Berakhot 55a.

[200] Proverbs 3:5, 7.

[201] Berakhot 55a.

[202] Berakhot 56a.

[203] Berakhot 55a.

[204] Zohar I, 183b.

[205] Genesis Rabba 89:8.

[206] *Shirah na'ah.*

[207] *Shinui ra.* The author quotes from Berakhot 56b.

[208] In his comments to Genesis 40:8.

[209] I.e., recite a certain prayer.

[210] Berakhot 55b.

[211] For the full text of these stories, see pp. 122–126 below.

[212] Moed Katan 28a. Actually, Rava was speaking not of himself but of Rabbah, an authority of the previous generation.

[213] The tefillin contain four passages from the Torah: Exodus 13:1–10, 11–16, Deuteronomy 6:4–9 and 11:13–21; apparently, one letter from Exodus 13:13 had been rubbed out.

[214] Thus invalidating them, with possible dire consequences.

[215] Berakhot 56a.

[216] I.e., and not according the interpretation(s) proposed above by R. Almoli.

[217] See Daniel 4:16 f.

[218] Daniel 4:24.

[219] A Spanish rabbi (1420–1494) who survived the expulsion from Spain and died in Naples; his best-known work is his commentary on the Humash, *Akedat Yitzhak.*

[220] Genesis 37:5.

[221] Zohar I, 183a–b.

[222] Genesis 41:13.

[223] A student of the great German talmudist, R. Asher b. Yehiel, who settled in Spain, and a colleague of the latter's son, R. Jacob, whom he quotes, R. Yose Ibn Nahamias lived in Toledo during the first half of the fourteenth century.

[224] One of the eight sons of R. Asher b. Yehiel, R. Jacob's legal code, the *Arba Turim,* became authoritative, serving as the basis of the *Shulhan Arukh,* and his Torah commentaries became widely used. He died before 1340.

[225] Lit., "sign," "token."

[226] Zohar I, 200a.

[227] Ibid. 7:14.

[228] Daniel 4:26.

[229] Presumably one of the constellations that represent animate beings, such as Virgo, Pisces, Taurus, Gemini, etc.

[230] I.e., Aquarius, but here the emphasis is on the inanimate part of the constellation, which represents a bucket, rather than on the water carrier.

²³¹ *Mazzalot,* "constellations," corrected from *ma'alot,* "degrees."

²³² As in the case of Gemini, the "Twins."

²³³ Exactly where the quotation begins is unclear, and so quotation marks have not been used.

²³⁴ Presumably some memory of having dreamed does remain with the dreamer, for otherwise he would have no need of an interpreter.

²³⁵ In Daniel 2.

²³⁶ See Daniel 2:1–12; Nebuchadnezzar refused to relate the dream to his interpreters, and his comment to Daniel in 2:26 implies that he could not recall it.

²³⁷ *Kol kakh meha-shanim.* Actually, the dream was fulfilled twelve months later, as reported in Daniel 4:26, and as R. Almoli himself notes above. Perhaps the phrase should be rendered "a certain amount [of time] of the years [to come]."

²³⁸ Recorded in Daniel 4.

²³⁹ Daniel 4:26.

²⁴⁰ Both of whom remembered their dreams and thus the dreams' fulfillment was immediate.

²⁴¹ Genesis 41:32.

²⁴² Joseph actually dreamed two dreams regarding his future rulership; see Genesis 37:5–11. R. Almoli may have considered them separate dreams with separate fulfillments, one foretelling Joseph's rise to power and his brothers' obeisance to him, and the second, his father's descent to Egypt.

²⁴³ I have been unable to identify this scholar or his work.

²⁴⁴ Many editions of Genesis Rabba 89:5, including current ones, end with the first sentence. R. Almoli's text contains an expanded version of the statement immediately preceding R. Yohanan's, but places it after R. Yohanan.

²⁴⁵ Genesis 41:5.

²⁴⁶ Daniel 2:1.

²⁴⁷ Genesis 37:2.

²⁴⁸ Genesis 41:46.

²⁴⁹ Berakhot 55b.

²⁵⁰ See Gersonides, *Wars of the Lord,* bk. II, chap. 7; in Feldman's translation, p. 70. However, Gersonides seems to hold out the possibility of prophetic dreams for the "distant future." See bk. II, chap. 6, in his discussion of the second objection; Feldman, p. 43.

²⁵¹ Yoma 76a.

²⁵² Berakhot 7a.

²⁵³ Berakhot, chap. 9.

²⁵⁴ That is, the Biblical Joseph.

255 Joseph, Daniel.

256 Deuteronomy 32:32.

257 The following "dream dictionary" has been slightly rearranged from the form in which it was given by R. Almoli. While the contents of each chapter remain the same, the order of the entries differs somewhat from R. Almoli's, and some combined entries have been separated. The version of this dictionary substantially follows that of Meir Bakal in his Jerusalem, 1965 quasi-edition of *Pitron Halomot Hashalem*.

258 From R. Hai Gaon.

259 Psalms 107:30.

260 Possibly referring to North Africa.

261 Since the Hebrew letter *beit* means "house."

262 R. Hai Gaon.

263 Berakhot 57a.

264 Isaiah 52:7.

265 Jeremiah 9:19. This is from the Talmud, Berakhot 56b.

266 This and the next interpretation are taken from the Talmud, Berakhot 57a.

267 A lesser office.

268 Which was used to announce the approach of an important person.

269 He subsequently became head of the yeshiva. The entire passage is from Berakhot 57a.

270 Taken from Rashi ad loc.

271 Genesis 26:19.

272 Proverbs 8:35.

273 Ibid.

274 Berakhot 56b.

275 Genesis 26:19.

276 Isaiah 59:19. This too is from Berakhot 56b.

277 See above.

278 Isaiah 66:12.

279 Isaiah 59:19. This is from Berakhot 56b.

280 Or: "will be sought out."

281 Berakhot 56b. The Talmud describes the person as "one who fears heaven with all his might."

282 Isaiah 38:14. This is the explanation given by Rashi; R. Nissim suggests that gourds are considered a sign of humility because they do not rise high above the ground.

283 Psalms 147:14.

284 Ibid. Berakhot 57a; in our editions, this reported in the name of R. Hiyya bar Abba.

285 The author seems to have quoted from memory, and confused matters a bit. The Talmud (Berakhot 57b) says: "All kinds of vegetables are a good [sign] in a dream, except turnip tops." "But did not Rav [not: R. Ashi] say: 'I did not become rich until I dreamed of turnip-tops?'" "When he saw them, it was in their stalks."

286 See above, s.v. vegetables: Others say: he will be well.

287 Presumably because grass is easy to find.

288 Cucumbers, kishuim in Hebrew, may be related to the word kasheh, "difficult, hard."

289 Generally speaking, however, garlic is considered a healthy food in the Talmud, and one which enhances fertility.

290 Isaiah 6:7.

291 Berakhot 57a.

292 In general, trees are taken to represent the person himself, as hinted in Deuteronomy 20:19, "is the man a tree of the field?"

293 Deuteronomy 20:19. The verse forbids cutting down fruit trees during a siege, on the grounds that the trees, in contrast to the people in the city, are not resisting the besiegers. According to this interpretation, trees are generally a bad omen because of this association. As the reader can see, this is a minority opinion.

294 In Talmudic and Rabbinic idiom, "trees" symbolize authoritative scholars.

295 Cedars symbolize strength in the Bible.

296 Berakhot 57a, citing Psalms 128:3.

297 Berakhot 57a, citing Genesis 49:11.

298 In our editions: "in a baraita."

299 Berakhot 57a.

300 Ibid. Just as the lulav has one stalk, so his heart is altogether given over to spiritual matters.

301 Berakhot 56a, citing Proverbs 4:5. The word kaneh, "reed," points to keneh, "acquire."

302 Ibid., citing Proverbs 4:7.

303 Isaiah 52:3.

304 Isaiah 36:6. In our editions of the Talmud the paragraphs are reversed.

305 Berakhot 57a, citing Proverbs 27:18.

306 Ibid., citing Leviticus 23:40.

307 Based on Berakhot 57a, regarding the nutritional worth of cherries, but not on dreaming about them.

308 Psalms 128:3.

309 Jeremiah 11:16.

310 Exodus 27:20.

311 Berakhot 57a.

312 See Avot 3:10.

313 Hosea 9:10.

314 Berakhot 56b, citing Deuteronomy 32:32.

315 The bracketed sentences are not in our editions of the Talmud, but are in some manuscripts; the author probably used a manuscript similar to one now in the Florence Library. This paragraph is also from Berakhot 56b, but not immediately after the previous one.

316 Berakhot 57b.

317 Song of Songs 8:2.

318 Ibid. 4:3.

319 Berakhot 57a.

320 Ibid., citing Lamentations 4:22; *tam*, "are at an end," and *tamar*, "date," sound alike.

321 Presumably wealth is a greater degree of prosperity than mere "property."

322 Psalms 104:15.

323 Proverbs 31:6.

324 Proverbs 9:5; the entire Talmudic passage is in Berakhot 57a.

325 Song of Songs 8:2. This last verse is not found in our editions, but seems to be taken from the Florence manuscript of the Talmud.

326 Exodus 27:20, cited in Berakhot 57a.

327 The Hebrew *yishmor nafsho mikol davar shema yippol* is ambiguous and may refer to either case.

328 Or: "miraculously."

329 Berakhot 57a.

330 Lit.: "father."

331 Proverbs 27:27.

332 Proverbs 27:27, cited in Berakhot 57a.

333 Berakhot 56b.

334 Deuteronomy 33:17.

335 Exodus 21:28. This Talmudic passage appears right before the one previously quoted.

336 Genesis 46:4.

337 II Samuel 12:13. This may relate the Hebrew word *gam*, "also" and *gamal*, "camel."

338 Zechariah 9:9, cited in Berakhot 56b.

[339] Berakhot 56b.

[340] Sanhedrin 93a.

[341] Habakkuk 3:8.

[342] The word *sus* is spelled with a *samekh*, while *sos* is spelled with a *sin*, both of which sound alike.

[343] Amos 3:8.

[344] Jeremiah 4:7.

[345] Berakhot 57a.

[346] As the serpent in Eden was cursed by being condemned to eat dust; see Genesis 3:14.

[347] *Pil* is "an elephant"; *pela'im* means "wonders."

[348] Berakhot 57a.

[349] *Shirah na'ah.*

[350] *Shinui ra.* The author quotes from Berakhot 56b.

[351] Exodus 11:7.

[352] Isaiah 56:11, cited in Berakhot 56b.

[353] Berakhot 57b.

[354] Proverbs 1:20.

[355] Berakhot 57a.

[356] Proverbs 27:8, cited in Berakhot 56a. The wandering presumably represents the punishment of exile, and so fasting is indicated.

[357] Proverbs 27:8, cited in Berakhot 56b. The exact quotation is: "R. Hanan said: 'There are three [kinds of dreams which symbolize] peace—a river, a bird, and a pot . . .' A bird because it is written, 'As birds hovering, so will God of Hosts protect Jerusalem.'" The verse is from Isaiah 31:5.

[358] Berakhot 57a.

[359] See Rashi ad loc. The acronym *nagol* = *na'e* and *gilah*, "pleasant" and "joy," respectively.

[360] I.e., they should not engage in too-frequent marital intercourse (see Berakhot 22a).

[361] Berakhot 57a. As in the case of rooster above, the word *tarnegolet*, "hen," is interpreted as an acronym: *tarbitza na'e* and *gilah*. *Tarbiza* can also refer to a courtyard in which a school meets (Rashi).

[362] As the ravens brought food to Elijah in the desert (I Kings 17:6).

[363] Genesis 40:17–22.

[364] Lit.: "fish."

[365] Berakhot 57a. Just as the contents of an egg are unknown until the shell is cracked open (Rashi).

[366] Ibid.

[367] The Hebrew *tishpot,* also meaning "place a pot on the fire."

[368] Isaiah 26:12.

[369] Ezekiel 24:3. Both interpretations are to be found in Berakhot 56b.

[370] Compare the expression "right-hand man."

[371] See also Berakhot 56b, where this is recorded as Rabbi Judah the Prince's interpretation of a dream of Bar Kappara's.

[372] For medicinal purposes.

[373] Berakhot 57a.

[374] Isaiah 1:18.

[375] Alluding to Gen 3:19.

[376] Isaiah 51:14.

[377] Berakhot 57a.

[378] Isaiah 51:14.

[379] Alluding to Genesis 3:19.

[380] When fasting is forbidden.

[381] Berakhot 57a.

[382] Genesis 41:14.

[383] Judges 16:17. This Talmudic reference is from Berakhot 56b.

[384] Berakhot 55a.

[385] When fasting is forbidden.

[386] In current editions: Rabbi [Judah the Prince].

[387] Since R. Eleazar had both.

[388] Berakhot 57b

[389] Ben Zoma attained knowledge of the mystical secrets of the Torah.

[390] Elisha b. Abuya, called Aher ("The Other One") because he became a Roman officer specializing in hunting down students of Torah.

[391] Berakhot 57b.

[392] That is, the Biblical Ishmael.

[393] Genesis 21:17.

[394] Berakhot 56b.

[395] Fol. 82b.

[396] Berakhot 57a. The Hebrew word for "miracle," *nes,* contains the letter *nun,* as does the name "Huna."

[397] Ibid.

[398] I, 168a.

[399] Who was a wicked king.

[400] Berakhot 57b.

[401] In his dream book.

[402] Berakhot 57a.

[403] Proverbs 7:4.
[404] Berakhot 57a.
[405] Proverbs 9:17.
[406] Deuteronomy 33:4.
[407] Berakhot 57a.
[408] This is probably a euphemism; if the Angel of Death is at your head or your feet. See Avodah Zarah 20b.
[409] In our editions: "peace in the house."
[410] In our editions: "it is a good sign for the house."
[411] Berakhot 57b.
[412] Berakhot 57b.
[413] Isaiah 1:18.
[414] I.e., it is a good sign. A similar interpretation is recorded in the Talmud, Berakhot 57a: Whoever sees himself tearing his clothes, his decree will be torn up. R. Almoli's statement may be a paraphrase of this, since the Florence manuscript of the Talmud, which he quotes elsewhere, does not here differ from our editions.
[415] In our editions: "In Babylon."
[416] Berakhot 57a.
[417] I Samuel 26:19.
[418] Ketubot 110b.
[419] Lit., "in."
[420] Presumably the stars represent the "hosts" of the army.
[421] Lit., "in."
[422] Genesis 1:3. The Talmudic statement is from Bava Kamma 55b.
[423] Berakhot 57a.
[424] Cantor.
[425] Of the lower grades.
[426] The second division of the Hebrew Bible.
[427] Jeremiah's message was one of hastening destruction.
[428] The third division of the Hebrew Bible.
[429] Song of Songs represents the spiritual relationship between God and the Jewish people, or between a man and his soul.
[430] Because it is the distillation of King Solomon's wisdom.
[431] Berakhot 57b.
[432] A scroll of the Law.
[433] When fasting is forbidden.
[434] This last phrase is not in our editions of the Talmud Berakhot, but seems to have been taken from Sukkah 28a.

435 Berakhot 57a.

436 Since Rosh Hashanah is Judgment Day.

437 Deuteronomy 28:10.

438 See Genesis 40:1–23.

439 Ibid. 49:9–11.

440 Ibid. 40:13.

441 See ibid. 40:16–17.

442 Ibid. 40:19.

443 "The wise know that even though two persons may dream the same dream, the interpreter must apply his knowledge of the dreamers and not interpret their dreams identically. For example, [just as] a horse may represent either wisdom or strength, so too if the dreamer is a wise man, and he dreams that he manages with great difficulty to cross a river while riding a horse, this denotes that he will overcome great obstacles by using his wisdom. However, if the dreamer is strong and valiant rather than wise, we should interpret the horse as representing strength [rather than wisdom]. . . . This [principle] is hidden from fools who claim knowledge of the science [of dream interpretation] but really know nothing about it."

444 See Judges 7:13.

445 Ibid. 7:14.

446 Berakhot 56a–b.

447 Deuteronomy 28:31.

448 Ibid. 28:41.

449 Ibid. 28:32.

450 Ibid. 28:32.

451 Kohelet 9:7.

452 Deuteronomy 28:38.

453 Ibid. 28:40.

454 Exodus 13:13.

455 See Song of Songs 5:2, where one's love is described as a dove.

456 That is, a miracle will happen to him but not to me; I will not be saved.

457 As in Genesis 22:17, 26:4, etc.

458 As in Genesis 22:17, 26:4, etc.

459 Lit., "quality."

460 Isaiah 29:8.

461 Zechariah 10:2.

462 Gittin 52a.

463 In the text: "That one." Either R. Manasseh was quoting from memory or he had a different version than that in our editions of the Talmud.

464 Both incidents are from Berakhot 56a.

465 Based on Zephaniah 3:13.

466 Genesis 20:6–7.

467 Ibid. 31:24.

468 Ibid. 40.

469 Daniel 2.

470 Ibid. 2:29.

471 Ibid. 2:30.

472 Berakhot 55b.

473 Berakhot 55b. That is, one does not see things which he generally does not think about.

474 A combination of dicta found in Berakhot 55a and 55b. A bad dream is sufficient in itself, without being fulfilled, since the sadness it brings leads to repentance. Likewise, continues R. Hisda, the joy a good dream brings is sufficient.

475 Shabbat 11b, Taanit 12b.

476 Based on Kohelet 7:20.

477 See Jonah 1:6.

478 Berakhot 55a.

479 Actually, he seems to be referring to Zohar Vayeshev (I 83a) or Vayehi (I 183a).

480 Hagigah 5a.

481 Berakhot 57b.

482 Genesis Rabba 17:5, 44:17–18.

483 Jeremiah 20:9.

484 The last clause is indecipherable; the translation follows the general sense.

485 Berakhot 55b; the exact text is: "R. Huna b. Ammi said in the name of R. Pedat in the name of R. Yohanan: If one has a dream which makes him sad, he should go and have it interpreted in the presence of three. Has not R. Hisda said: A dream which is not interpreted is like a letter which is not read? Say rather: He should have it favorably interpreted in the presence of three."

486 Numbers 12:6.

487 Zechariah 10:2.

488 Berakhot 55b.

489 Genesis 41:8.

490 Daniel 2:1.

491 Isaiah 38:1.

492 Calling Isaiah by his father's name as a sign of his displeasure.

493 That is, there must be some good in the decree you have just delivered to

me; prayer will still help! The entire story is to be found in Berakhot 10a.

494 Kohelet 3:14.

495 See Berakhot 57a for the source of the last statement.

496 Lit., "the great panic awakens him."

497 That is, he is awakened from a doze and falls back into it; finally he decides to go to sleep for the night.

498 Song of Songs 5:2.

499 Referring to the custom of *kapparot* before Yom Kippur, and thus implying that the dreamer requires atonement.

500 Presumably all signs of mourning, implying that the dreamer or one close to him will soon die.

501 Since the demon only intends to frighten the dreamer, and these are not true angelic dreams.

502 A euphemism: they hear about an evil decree passed regarding that person.

503 Signifying that they are now in the Heavenly Academy.

504 Referring to all the great figures mentioned above, and others like them.

505 So that he does not suspect that he is being shown a demonic dream.

506 Prayers for the coming of the Messiah and the restoration of the Temple.

507 Ritual bath.

508 All these are intended to raise him to a state of purity so that he may be taught mystical secrets of the Torah.

509 The verse quoted is written in Aramaic, and was sent by Elijah to the exiles in Babylonia.

510 Of God.

511 As we know from the Book of Kings; see I Kings 17:1, for example.

512 And since he had not returned, it is clear that he kept his oath, even where Elijah the Prophet might not have. This somewhat surprising deduction is the only way to understand what follows.

513 Lit., "with a very tenuous hint."

514 Genesis 37:5–10.

515 Daniel 2:1–45.

516 Numbers 5:27.

517 That is, they correspond to Israel but on the "left side," the sinister, evil side.

518 Who represents the Arabs and Muslims.

519 A high priest is permitted to involve himself with his wife's burial, even though he is made ritually impure by contact with a dead body. In this case, Rabbi Ftayya hinted to the man that he ought not to involve himself because she was no longer his wife; a priest's wife who has relations with another man *must* be divorced, even if the circumstances were not adulterous.

[520] "Table" is used as a euphemism for marital relations in the Talmud; see Nedarim 20b.

[521] With his sons; presumably this refers to the custom of remaining awake all night and studying in preparation for the celebration of the giving of the Torah the next morning. As will become apparent, the scholar had three sons.

[522] Ordinarily it is forbidden to fast on the Sabbath; a fast to mitigate the evil effects of a dream is permitted, though it must later be atoned for.

[523] The image of flames of love is found in the Zohar, Raya Mehemna, Tzav, 33a.

[524] The image of two thighs, referring to the loving brothers Zebulun and Issachar, is also found in the Zohar, II 104b.

[525] Applying Numbers 12:3 to the physician's father.

[526] Or: "an elder."

[527] Presumably the ritual shawl worn during prayers.

[528] Alluding to Psalms 109:11.

[529] After which they ascend to their heavenly rest.

[530] Deuteronomy 8:3.

[531] At creation, when God poured of His own essence into vessels that were intended to contain this light but could not. This resulted in a cosmic catastrophe, the "breaking of the vessels," which were unable to contain the infinite plenitude of the En-Sof. The overflow of "sparks" fell into a variety of *kelipot,* or "shells"—symbols of matter, the nondivine, the potential for evil—where they were "captured" and await "redemption" or liberation by man by means of his service of the Lord, especially the performance of the mitzvot, the study of Torah, and Kabbalistic meditations. Among these is the recital of blessings.

[532] Psalms 109:17.

[533] There are four pieces of parchment in a phylactery, on each of which is written one of the four following passages from the Torah: Exodus 13:1–10, 11–16; Deuteronomy 6:4–9, 11:13–21.

[534] The system by which each Hebrew letter is assigned a numeric value; by this means, words with identical numeric values are in some sense related.

[535] The four-letter Name of God, *yod-he-vav-he*: $10 + 5 + 6 + 5 = 26$. Multiplied five times, this yields 130.

[536] And that is why he saw his father's eye plucked out.

[537] Certainly an inappropriate action.

[538] One of the honors given at a Brith; it is considered propitious for having children. Since Elijah is considered "the Angel of the Brith," a "throne" is set for him.

[539] From Proverbs 1:5.